The Legacy of Tiananmen Square

Also by MICHEL CORMIER

Richard Hatfield: Power and Disobedience (with Achille Michaud)

Louis J. Robichaud: A Not So Quiet Revolution

The Legacy of
TIANANMEN
SQUARE

MICHEL
CORMIER

Translated by JONATHAN KAPLANSKY

GOOSE LANE

Goose Lane Editions acknowledges the
generous support of the Canada Council
for the Arts, the Government of Canada
through the Canada Book Fund (CBF), and
the Government of New Brunswick through
the Department of Tourism, Heritage,
and Culture.

Translated with the support of the Banff
International Literary Translation Centre
(BILTC) at The Banff Centre, Banff, Alberta,
Canada.

Goose Lane Editions
500 Beaverbrook Court, Suite 330
Fredericton, New Brunswick
CANADA E3B 5X4
www.gooselane.com

Cover and interior images: "Flags at Tiananmen
Square" by Cronocious, Deviantart.com; and
"Tiananmen Square" by WrappedUpInBooks,
Deviantart.com
Cover and page design by Julie Scriver.
Printed in Canada.
10 9 8 7 6 5 4 3 2 1

Library and Archives Canada Cataloguing in
Publication

Cormier, Michel, 1957-
The legacy of Tiananmen Square / Michel Cormier;
translated by Jonathan Kaplansky.

Translation of: Les héritiers de Tiananmen.
Includes bibliographical references and index.
Issued also in electronic format.

ISBN 978-0-86492-902-0

1. China — Politics and government — 1949-.
I. Title.

DS777.75.C6713 2013   951.05
C2012-907163-3

To my sons, Philippe, Dominique, and Samuel

Contents

Prologue

An overnight snowfall has blanketed Beijing, and Xi Xin Zhu struggles to find the site of his former home, of which only the foundation remains. He stops, looks up, finds a landmark, and sets off again, this time to the left. Beneath the snow, the ground is muddy. The neighbourhood where Xi Xin Zhu lived in West Beijing is now a vast wasteland, flattened to make way for luxury villas. The Summer Palace, where the emperors of China went to escape the heat of the capital, can be seen in the distance. "That's part of the reason real estate developers wanted to get a hold of this property," Zhu tells me, "because of the view of the Summer Palace." The expropriation and demolition notices were delivered on the same day, a Friday. Xi Xin Zhu and his family had until the following Monday to leave the premises. He considered the compensation he was offered unacceptable. And he didn't see what gave them the right to demolish his house to build villas. He tried to appeal, but the municipality's offices are closed on weekends. So Xi Xin Zhu decided to resist. He sent his wife and children to stay with relatives and barricaded himself inside the house. When the demolition workers arrived on Monday, Xi Xin Zhu tried to reason with them but to no avail. The power shovel moved in to take the first bite out of his property. But he couldn't bring himself to watch the destruction of what he'd spent twenty years building. Desperate, Zhu doused himself with gasoline and set himself on fire. The workers intervened, called for help, then got back to their job. Xi Xin Zhu was rescued from the flames, but his house was destroyed, as planned.

Several months later he met me outside the hospital where he was still recovering to tell me his story and take me to what remains of his property. His scalp and part of his face are burned, as are both his hands. One hand is covered with a gauze dressing. The pain is still intense. Continuing his search, he finds the foundation of his former home. A low wall, about thirty centimetres high, can be detected beneath the snow. He opens his cellphone with difficulty and shows me the pictures of his house. "This is what they destroyed," he says. "They had no right. But they're in league with one another, the authorities and the developers. They do whatever they like." Xi Xin Zhu went to court to try to have the expropriation order reversed. The judge refused to hear his case. Worse, he was accused of disturbing public order after he tried to stop demolition workers from doing their work. For illegally opposing the party's will.

Like millions of Chinese, Xi Xin Zhu felt he had laid part of the foundation of the new China. He had heeded the call of Deng Xiaoping, who at the end of the 1980s had urged the Chinese to get rich. The patriarch had thereby removed the economic shackles of Mao-style socialism and launched China on the road to its spectacular economic ascent. Xi Xin Zhu had opened a small furniture workshop. Over the years, the business had grown and he had saved enough to build a house for himself and his family on an attractive property in the western part of the capital. But his dream ended brutally when the authorities decided to seize the property and hand it over to developers. Today, the burns on his hands prevent Xi Xin Zhu from making furniture. Standing in the snow, hands aching with cold, he swears he won't give up. "My spirit is still intact," he tells me. But deep down he knows he has no recourse.

Xi Xin Zhu's story is the hidden face of China's economic miracle, of the China that managed to pull off the most spectacular economic transformation in the twentieth century, even as it upheld its authoritarian state. A China that not only offers little recourse to its citizens but also often brutalizes people who are victims of injustice, corruption, or even natural disasters. All those, in other words, whose grievances are liable to contradict the image of the harmonious society the Chinese government wishes the world to see. In almost five years of journalism in China, I have seen this face many times. I've seen it on the woman who lived in utter poverty at the bottom of a chemical wasteland in what in China is called a cancer village. The factory overlooking her property on a tributary of the Yangtze River specialized in chemicals used in making computer screens and mobile phones. She'd turned up her pant leg to show me the lesion that appeared on her calf after her exposure to toxic waste. Even after seven years, it hadn't healed. She, too, had complained to the authorities. She, too, was accused of disturbing the peace. It is the face of the mother who lost her daughter when a poorly built school collapsed during the Sichuan earthquake. She'd agreed to meet me on a country road to talk about her anger at the authorities who wanted to silence her. Her phone had been tapped. When we met, she barely had time to greet me before plainclothes police officers got out of three unmarked cars and took her away by force. It is the face of the man who had come from northern China just before the Olympics, believing he could demonstrate to get answers about his daughter's suspicious death in a military barracks. But he was refused permission to demonstrate. He'd set up a meeting with us in Tiananmen Square, where he unfurled a banner demanding justice. He, too, was immediately taken away by plainclothes police officers. It is the face of Zhao Lianhai, who wanted to set up an organization for parents of children poisoned by melamine-contaminated milk and was sentenced to two and a half years in prison for disturbing the peace. His crime: demanding an independent inquiry into the scandal.

The China that combines economic freedom with the state's hard line is the China that emerged from the Tiananmen crisis. In 1989, confronted with hundreds of thousands of people in Tiananmen Square demanding democratic reforms, the Communist Party found itself at a crossroads. It chose to repress the student movement. The idea of democracy was crushed under the treads of the tanks. Chinese leaders concluded that not only could the new market economy approach co-exist with political authoritarianism but its success depended on this approach. The China that emerged from this situation is one where political leaders are answerable only to themselves, justice is arbitrary, and expressions of political freedom are harshly repressed. Today, China may be the second-largest world economic power, but it is also one of the most corrupt countries in the world.

In universities and Western capitals we often hear that the democratization of China is inevitable and that establishing a market economy in China will necessarily lead to democracy. This argument no longer holds water. China is proving that capitalism and political authoritarianism are more compatible than people would like to believe. Chinese authorities, in the wake of the 2010 Nobel Peace Prize win by Liu Xiaobo, one of its imprisoned dissidents, claimed that democracy and human rights are not universal values but rather a new expression of Western imperialism. Their position on this matter could not be clearer. Current Chinese leaders not only consider the establishment of a political system in which the Chinese people would choose their governance from multiple political parties as undesirable for China but also view this as running counter to the interests, indeed to the very nature, of their society.

Does this mean that China is too densely populated to sustain a democracy or that its development is too fragile to allow the Chinese to choose their leaders? That China's very culture, particularly its tradition of filial obedience, is incompatible with the idea of democracy, that the Chinese are meant to be governed by the modern equivalent of an emperor? Quite the contrary. Such reasoning denies both reality and history. The Chinese people have constantly yearned for a government answerable for its actions. The idea that the sovereign must earn the people's trust was at the heart of Confucian philosophy. Even before the American and French revolutions, before the advent of accountable government in Great Britain, the emperors of China recognized that their power, which took the form of a "Mandate of Heaven," could legitimately be revoked if they did not satisfy the needs of the people. This idea fuelled peasant revolts that threatened dynasties and inspired reformers throughout the twentieth century, from the first attempt to found a republic after the fall of the Qing Dynasty in 1912 to the demonstrations in Tiananmen Square in 1989. This same thirst for justice drives hundreds of thousands of Chinese to take to the streets each year not necessarily to demand a Western-style right to vote but greater accountability from their government. It is this refusal to bend to arbitrary methods that leads Chinese such as Xi Xin Zhu to denounce a government that took his house and against which he is powerless.

The reasons why China has not become democratic are varied and complex. This book aims to explore the political, historical, and cultural obstacles that might shed light on why China is one of the world's few major countries not to commit to an elected government. In it, I will assess the effects on China of more than a century of failed attempts at democratization. This is not a plea for or against democracy, nor an academic study. It is a kind of in-depth reporting about the debate on democracy in China, and as such, it is a work of journalism more than of history or political science. Each chapter looks at a significant milestone in this history through the eyes of the people who have lived through it. It is a project that led me to delve into history books to find out what motivated the first activists for democracy at the turn of the twentieth century. An endeavour that took me from New York to Washington, from London to Hong Kong, where I met exiled activists of more recent campaigns: the Democracy Wall of 1978 and the Tiananmen movement. It took me into the living rooms of disgraced former Chinese leaders who, twenty years after their unsuccessful attempt to launch China on the path of democratic reform, still live under house arrest, prisoners in their own apartments. It took me to the doors of the tribunals that condemned contemporary democracy activists — those referred to as cyber-dissidents — to heavy prison sentences. And it led me to meet members of the Charter 08 movement, who paid dearly for their attempt to revive the debate on democracy in the wake of the 2008 Olympic Games.

Why should we be interested in China's relationship with democracy at a time when the question seems almost outdated? Because the question of China's unfulfilled political reforms is important. The lack of accountability of Chinese authorities has led to widespread corruption that undermines China's economic miracle.

Moreover, the way in which China governs itself will have repercussions not only on the Chinese but also on the rest of the world. China is no longer

Asia's poor relation struggling to feed its population. It is the new giant in the world economy, a powerhouse that is beginning to export its political values and development model to other areas of the globe. Its model, which successfully combines economic liberalism and political authoritarianism, is becoming an alternative, even a competitor, to the Western model of industrial and political development. In many respects, this Chinese model stems from the Chinese authorities' decision, in June 1989, to quell the momentum of political reform in Tiananmen Square. Our saga, which will explore these tragic and decisive events, begins with those days in June 1989 that helped set China on its current path.

1

Wang Juntao's Exile

New York, December 2008

Wang Juntao arranges to meet me at a Starbucks at the corner of Broadway and 111th Street, across from Columbia University, his university pied-à-terre in Manhattan. I offer to rent a car and meet him at his home in New Jersey. "You might get lost," he tells me on the phone. "In any case, I have things to do at the university." He speaks warmly, as if we've known each other a long time. "How will I know you?" he adds. "I'm sure I'll recognize you," I reply. After all, Wang Juntao is one of the best known Chinese dissidents. Considered by the Chinese government as one of the "black hands" behind the Tiananmen student movement, he was condemned to thirteen years in prison, the most severe sentence imposed in the wake of the spring crisis of 1989 in Beijing. Freed for medical reasons in 1994 on the eve of American president Bill Clinton's visit to China, he has since been living in exile in the United States.

The intellectual and reformer arrives on the dot at the appointed hour, briefcase slung across his shoulder. He gets to the counter ahead of me and offers to pay for coffee. "It's the least I can do for someone who is interested in China's future," he says. We sit at the last available table, near the window. Outside, passersby brace themselves against a December wind. The sky is the colour of steel. I put the tape recorder on the table and ask Wang Juntao to tell me about Tiananmen.

"On the evening of June 3, 1989," he says, "I was to meet, as I did every day, the student leaders for our daily strategy meeting. I showed up at the hotel where we had our headquarters, not far from Tiananmen Square, but no one was there. I sent my driver to see what was going on. He returned, telling me the army was advancing toward the square. I ran over. I knew it was the end. My only objective was to save the student leaders from the massacre that would take place. To do so, we had to leave Beijing. I left to look for them with my chauffeur. There were huge crowds everywhere."

At Tiananmen Square, few protesters were left. Many, faced with the rumour of military intervention, had gone back home. The student leaders who were still there decided, in a last stand, to take an oath to the cause they had been defending for more than a month. They knew their struggle for democracy was lost. Already, the tanks of the People's Army were advancing toward the square; in the distance shots could be heard. Deng Xiaoping, patriarch of the Communist regime, had decided to put an end to the student revolt. West of the city, in the working-class neighbourhoods, hundreds, perhaps thousands, of civilians, believing that the army would not fire on the people, fell to the bullets of soldiers or died crushed under the tracks of the tanks.

"We swear to protect the cause of Chinese democracy," the students proclaimed in unison. "We aren't afraid to die. We don't want to keep on living in a troubled country. We will protect Tiananmen to the bitter end. Down with Li Peng's military rule!" The square, in which a few days earlier close to a million demonstrators had gathered, now contained only a few thousand. The ground was littered with tents and debris. Resigned to martyrdom, the students awaited the final assault.

The army had difficulty advancing, however. People seemed determined to prevent the soldiers from reaching Tiananmen Square. Ordinary citizens erected makeshift barricades by placing buses crosswise in the street. A labour union distributed shovels and pickaxes to its members. Some of them knocked down the wall of a building site to allow people to arm themselves with bricks and stones. On Fuxing Road, a main artery several kilometres to the west of Tiananmen Square, thousands of people formed a human chain to block the army's advance. The government, doubting the loyalty of the soldiers camped in Beijing, had called up detachments from the provinces, who were considered more obedient. They fired warning shots. But the human chain refused to back down. The soldiers then fired into the crowd. They even fired on the ambulance personnel who tried to assist the wounded. At Fuxing Hospital, there were no longer enough doctors to treat everyone transported there by makeshift means, on bicycles, motorcycles, or even on doors used as stretchers. Inexorably, the military continued its march to "free" Tiananmen Square. The crowd drew back but showed no mercy to the soldiers when it managed to get its hands on them. Two soldiers who tried to extricate themselves from a tank set afire by Molotov cocktails were beaten to death. In a brutal burst of violence, the crowd clubbed the skull of one of the soldiers open.

Around one o'clock in the morning on June 4, the army finally surrounded Tiananmen Square. The military used loudspeakers to tell protesters it had orders to put an end to the protest. The government branded the occupation an anti-revolutionary movement, which is tantamount to treason according to Chinese political vocabulary. A few students tried to convince the soldiers to put down their weapons; one of them was killed point-blank. The determination of the student leaders wavered. Those who, a few hours before, swore to die rather than to give up were not driven by the same hatred or the same courage as the workers or ordinary people who barred the soldiers' way at the cost of their lives. The students didn't believe it would come to this. When they began to demonstrate, in May, after the death of the reformer and former chairman Hu Yaobang, it was to call for the end of corruption and more transparency in the party. No one dreamed of overthrowing the regime. They even believed they had the support of Zhao Ziyang, the general secretary of the party and second-in-command in the regime after Deng Xiaoping.

Chai Ling, nicknamed the Joan of Arc of the student movement, addressed the last protesters gathered around the Monument to the People's Heroes. "Those who want to leave should go," she told the group, "and those who want to stay, stay." While the elite troops, assault rifles at the ready, advanced toward them, the students voted with a show of hands. A majority decided to leave. Not far from there, Liu Xiaobo, a young academic and literary critic who had returned home from the United States to take part in the Tiananmen Square movement, had begun a hunger strike two days earlier with three other activists, one of whom was a young rock singer. Determined to prevent what seemed like an imminent massacre, he stepped in to mediate between the army and the students. Thanks to his intervention, the military agreed to let the students go. Escorted by the soldiers, they left the square singing "The Internationale" and calling the soldiers animals and fascists. In an absurd parody of their struggle, the effigy of the American Statue of Liberty they had erected across from Mao's portrait was unceremoniously knocked over by a tank. Some students were arrested; others managed to flee, leaving the country. China's democratic spring ended in blood, humiliation, and escape.

Wang Juntao knew that to survive the military crackdown spreading through the capital, he and the student leaders had to leave Beijing as soon as possible. In the confusion and panic, he still needed two days to find everyone. "I didn't know what was going to happen, but I was certain of one thing," he tells me. "If we wanted to stay alive, we had to leave Beijing as quickly as possible. At that moment the situation was very fluid. It was even possible that elements of the armed forces in favour of our struggle would rebel and organize a coup. We had to be ready for any eventuality." On the morning of June 7, they left by train, heading to the northeast, barely avoiding a huge search operation that would sweep the capital. Within a few days, their photos would be put up in train stations and other public places. They were part of the twenty-one people most wanted for their role in the Tiananmen Square protests.

Wang Juntao, Wang Dan, and two other students managed to reach Shanghai. They thought that by being in the city they would more easily melt into the background. But the police were everywhere. Feeling more vulnerable in a group, they separated. Wang Juntao tried to reach southern China in the hope of secretly entering Hong Kong. Betrayed by one of the smugglers in the network, he was arrested in a train station while trying to buy a ticket. Wang Juntao was brought back to Beijing in handcuffs. Then came his trial, followed by prison, and his sudden and unexpected liberation a few days before the visit of American president Bill Clinton. Since then,

Wang Juntao has built a new life for himself in the American academic world. Once his passport expired, he was no longer considered to be a Chinese citizen. He is still not allowed back in his country. But his dream of a democratic China remains intact.

More than twenty years later, the legacy of Tiananmen Square remains, an unsolved problem. The prominent names in the struggle, such as Wang Juntao, the mentor of the student leaders, or Wang Dan, leader of the Tiananmen student movement, live for the most part in exile in the United States, Europe, Hong Kong, or Taiwan. Their voices, for all practical purposes, have been stilled. In continental China, the struggle for democratization only survives underground. Any discussion on the country's political future outside the framework of the Communist Party is severely repressed. In such a context, what remains of the democratic ideal in which so many Chinese believed during the spring of 1989? What do they think today of their battle and of the prospects for democratization of a China that managed to carry out one of the most spectacular economic U-turns in history while officially staying the course of its unfinished socialist revolution? What are China's real prospects for democratization at a time when democracy has such bad press, given the parody it has become in the former USSR and the difficulties experienced by the West in making democratic reforms take hold in Iraq and Afghanistan? Should the struggle for democracy still be a priority for Chinese reformers, or must they first work at building a civil society and a rule of law capable of making democracy effective if and when it finally takes hold? These are questions that inhabit the daily lives of the exiled veterans of the Tiananmen movement and of those who still fight for political reform in China.

Today, the term *Tiananmen Square* remains a powerful symbol whose meaning varies diametrically depending on Western or Chinese points of view. For a good part of the international community, Tiananmen Square represents the symbol of a regime that chose to sacrifice the prime of its youth rather than accept change. The iconic image of a young man standing in the way of a line of tanks in the days following the massacre now appears for Westerners alongside scenes such as that of the Prague Spring in the gallery of pictures of twentieth-century Communist repression. But Tiananmen Square is also the battle for the triumph of liberal democracy, the inevitability of which many thinkers, especially in the United States, predicted with the fall of the Berlin Wall and the subsequent collapse of the Soviet empire. Today, Tiananmen Square is still to a large extent the prism through which the West sees China. When Western leaders travel to Beijing and mention China's human rights record in the presence of Chinese leaders, the unfinished business of Tiananmen Square is perceptible, both as a kind of uneasiness and remorse. The fact that the West keeps repeating the mantra that the market economy will bring about China's democratization implicitly refers to the unresolved issue of Tiananmen Square.

Conversely, for China and its leaders, Tiananmen Square remains both a trauma and a taboo. The lesson Communist leaders learned from it is that opening the door to political reforms outside the limited framework of the party threatens the regime's very survival. To understand the fear that the prospect of democratization inspires in them, we have to return to the context that led to the events of Tiananmen Square.

In the 1980s, Mao's successor, Deng Xiaoping, had not only begun economic liberalization of the country but also allowed extensive discussion of the political reforms that were to accompany the transition to a market economy. This unexpected opening spawned discussion groups, journals, and magazines, and a committee was even set up to study various reform scenarios within the government. When the students took to the streets and occupied Tiananmen Square, their initial aim was to show support for Zhao Ziyang, the reformist general secretary who was fighting a conservative backlash within the politburo. *The Tiananmen Papers,* published in 2001 in the United States by two renowned American sinologists, Andrew Nathan and Perry Link, tells the story of the deep divisions within the Chinese leadership during the spring of 1989.[1] The book consists of a series of reports, transcripts, and accounts of conversations from the highest spheres of the Communist regime smuggled out of China after the massacre. They allow the reader to follow the day-to-day discussions, divisions, and positions of the government throughout the spring of 1989 and up to the days following the military intervention that put an end to the student protest.

These papers reveal the extent to which Deng Xiaoping was torn between the inclination to let the students express themselves and the reflex to quell their demonstrations. In the end, the old revolutionary could not come to terms with the idea that these youths, with the support of a significant portion of the population, could question not only the heritage of the Communist revolution but also, to some extent, the legitimacy of the regime.

In the fateful weeks leading to the bloody outcome of Tiananmen Square, Wang Juntao believed he was in a position to find a compromise between the students and the government and manufacture an agreement that would allow Chinese leaders to save face and the demonstrators to return home with their heads held high. At the time, Wang Juntao was one of the rising intellectual stars in China but also acted as an informal link to the reformist wing of the Communist leadership. Wang owed his notoriety to the fact that he had gone to prison for taking part in demonstrations commemorating the death of Zhou Enlai in 1976. He was only sixteen at the time. With his liberation and consequent rehabilitation, he became a symbol in China. To show how ready it was to make way for the reformers and victims of the purges of the Mao era, the new leadership of the party appointed Wang to the Central Committee of the Communist Youth League. Wang, however, continued to act in many capacities. In 1978 he became one of the most active but also moderate activists of the Democracy Wall. He launched, with others, the journal *Beijing Spring*, a scarcely veiled reference to the Prague Spring. People who contributed to it did not directly challenge the power of the Communist Party but campaigned for socialism with a human face.[2] They called for respecting the rights guaranteed by the constitution, particularly freedom of the press, an essential condition for keeping the party on the straight and narrow.

Wang Juntao was not only the most famous of the activists for democracy but also, with his friend and partner Chen Zeming, one of the few who had succeeded in business. The two embodied the spirit of the times when people could have ideas and make money, and even make money with ideas. They owned their own research institute and the first private polling firm in China. Chen used the profits he made with two correspondence course schools to buy, together with Wang, an economic research institute connected to the Academy of Sciences. They renamed it the Beijing Social and Economic Sciences Research Institute. This privatization of knowledge and analysis was a first in China. They carried out studies for public or private clients, published books, and conducted opinion polls on subjects as sensitive as the political attitudes of the Chinese. Starting in 1988, they also published a review that became very popular with young Chinese in which they tackled the themes of democracy and reform. According to Wang Juntao, the fact that their institute was financially independent from the government was crucial. "Since we owned a business, no one could control what we published: so we had complete freedom of expression." Their institute rapidly became the crossroads for many reform proposals and ensured that Wang Juntao and Chen Zeming played a key role in the reformist discussion that swept over China at the end of the 1980s.

In contrast with others, who wanted to carry out a French-style revolution, Wang and Chen dreamed of a British-style transition, "where we would come to a new arrangement with the king; we weren't interested in drastic change," says Wang Juntao. In their opinion, for democracy to work, it had to be supported by a civil society, institutions, and a rule of law. Demanding democracy without first laying the groundwork for it to function would lead to failure. In the course of their discussions, Wang and Chen reached an important observation: they wanted to be agents of change, not simply political agitators. To do so, they had to propose practical, pragmatic ideas on the reforms and cultivate alliances outside, but above all, inside the government. "If you want to have influence in China," says Wang Juntao, "you must have a network inside the system and be connected to independent groups outside the government. That was our strategy."

Wang and Chen worked at gathering together all those who wanted to change China: the intellectuals, students, journalists, and new entrepreneurs interested in politics. They organized seminars and published articles and books, all with the goal of creating a hub of reform in Chinese society. "Our intention was to build a political base for change," says Wang. "To bring together all the independent thinkers and create public opinion in China." Ideally, they would have liked to establish a political party, but that was impossible in Deng's China. For want of anything better, Wang said, their institute became a kind of informal party. Considering his notoriety, it is completely natural that Wang Juntao found himself in the heart of the events of Tiananmen Square in the spring of 1989. He quickly became, with his friend Chen Zeming, one of the éminences grises of the student movement. But he also had close ties with reformers inside the government, notably Bao Tong, the assistant of General Secretary Zhao Ziyang, who led the committee on political reform appointed by Deng Xiaoping.

In the beginning, there was something festive about the demonstrations. Up to a million people would assemble in Tiananmen Square. But Wang Juntao knew that the spontaneity of the student movement was also his Achilles heel and that the hard-liners around Deng Xiaoping would not tolerate such an affront forever. "The problem with the student leaders," he told me, "was that they didn't have specific demands that could have led to a negotiated compromise. They demanded more transparency from the government, the end of corruption, and a vague idea of democracy. I knew then that negotiation was basically impossible. Reformists inside the government said so to me: 'But what do they want? Make a list, then we can have a discussion.' That had become impossible."

At the end of May, the situation became critical. General Secretary Zhao Ziyang, the leader of the reformist camp, was arrested. Li Peng, the prime minister and new strongman of the regime, had just proclaimed martial law. Soldiers began to move into the outskirts of the capital. Wang Juntao knew that little time remained to defuse the crisis. But he also knew that the students themselves were divided. The moderate wing, represented by

Wang Dan, a young history student who knew how to stir up crowds, wanted to free Tiananmen Square and avoid military intervention. He believed that the students had won a moral victory and to continue the demonstrations would jeopardize whatever gains they had made. With dozens of other students he had staged a hunger strike that had crystallized Chinese opinion in their favour. The more radical wing of the movement, however, refused to withdraw.

Wang Juntao was also very much aware it would be impossible to convince the hundreds of thousands of students who had been demonstrating for a month in Tiananmen Square to go home without winning concessions from the government. They were intoxicated by their struggle, by the support of the people, and by the notoriety they had outside China. On the morning of May 27, Wang Juntao, his colleague Chen Zeming, and other liberals met with the student leaders. They thought they'd found a way out of the crisis. They suggested that the students adopt a resolution demanding a special session of the People's Congress, the Chinese parliament that meets once a year. Congress had the power to revoke the martial law that had just been imposed and that was responsible for a significant escalation of tension. Wang and Chen hoped that this would allow for a return to calm and for a better climate for negotiation. In exchange, the demonstrators would agree to free Tiananmen Square. After long discussions, Chai Ling, the representative of the radical wing of the student movement, finally agreed to their proposal. Wang Juntao was relieved; the worst, he believed, had been avoided. Chai Ling said she would personally take care of informing the demonstrators of the decision. But once in Tiananmen Square, she could not bring herself to announce the end of the battle. She rallied those who demanded pursuing the struggle to the end. One week later, Deng Xiaoping gave the order to the military to put an end to the demonstrations. Wang Juntao became an outlaw; his photo was put up in public places as one of the most wanted men in China.

★ ★ ★

The campaign of Wang Juntao and of other activists in the Tiananmen Square movement in the spring of 1989 was the last in a long series of battles to democratize China that ended in failure. There was the Hundred Days' Reform, when intellectuals tried to introduce democratic reforms to the Qing court at the end of the nineteenth century; the establishment of the short-lived elected government in 1912, overthrown almost immediately by the generals; the Movement of May 4, 1919, which saw intellectuals occupy Tiananmen Square to demand China's democratic and scientific modernization; the Hundred Flowers Campaign at the end of the 1950s, when the Chinese were invited by Mao to express criticisms of the Communist Party before being severely repressed; the Democracy Wall of 1978, on which Chinese from all different backgrounds posted their demands for a more open China; and finally Tiananmen Square, ten years later, the peak of a century's struggle for democracy. All the protagonists of these struggles inherited the battle of those who came before. But their cause, tossed about on the rough seas of China's twentieth century, foundered each time before reaching port.

The catastrophic conclusion of the events of Tiananmen Square has had significant and unpredictable consequences for China. Many sinologists believe that Chinese leaders came to the conclusion that to temper the thirst for political reform, the pace of economic reforms had to be accelerated. Deng Xiaoping's historic visit to the new economic zone of Shenzhen in 1992 was considered symbolic of this. It would be the initial spark of the economic big bang that launched China on its spectacular economic trajectory. Some analysts go even further and claim that the economic reforms of the past twenty years were actually a substitute for political reforms. The Chinese regime thus "reached the stage of governance without first going through the stage of democracy."[3] This governance, in the case of China today, consists of managing the problems of the new market economy, which excludes any political discussion. According to this logic, calling the Chinese political system into question is tantamount to questioning the legitimacy of economic progress and refusing to grant the Chinese the advantages of a consumer society. The only discussion allowed concerns improving the way the system works and must have as its premise the perpetuity of the Communist regime.

At a time when the majority of Chinese aspire — legitimately, needless to say — to the benefits of development, democracy activists see themselves relegated to the catacombs of dissidence. They lead their battle mainly on the Internet or in publications outside China, thus exposing themselves to severe reprisals that sometimes can go as far as imprisonment. The most prominent recent case is that of Liu Xiaobo, the literary critic who negotiated safe conduct with the army, allowing student leaders to leave Tiananmen Square before being subjected to an attack by the military in the early hours of June 4, 1989. Liu was one of the few Chinese intellectuals and veterans of this campaign to remain in China to continue the struggle for democratization. His last initiative, the Charter 08 movement, which demanded free elections, earned him an eleven-year prison sentence but also brought him the 2010 Nobel Peace Prize. Chinese authorities, traumatized by the memory of hundreds of thousands of youths in Tiananmen Square demanding reforms, nip in the bud any hint of campaigns that could lead the Chinese to demand changes to the political regime.

In this context it isn't surprising that Chinese authorities have erased the events of Tiananmen Square from history books and collective memory. Any political discussion of the June 1989 movement, which the government still describes as a counter-revolution, is forbidden; any research of the question on the Internet is automatically blocked. Few Chinese born after Tiananmen Square have heard of it. A young staff member of a Sichuan newspaper was fired a few years ago because he had authorized publication of a text by the Tiananmen Mothers, the women who lost children during the massacre and who to this day demand justice. The young journalist believed that Tiananmen Square referred to an ancient military battle.

It's as if all of China had been struck with collective amnesia. But that's not all. A large part of the intelligentsia that inspired the political reform movement at the time of Tiananmen has joined the ranks of technocratic governance. These intellectuals have accepted the new role the regime offered them, a role that "consists in bringing their technical expertise to the government to allow it to carry out the modernization of the country."[4] In exchange for this influence, the intellectuals implicitly agree not to question the legitimacy of the Communist Party.

From his prison cell, at the beginning of the 1990s, Wang Juntao saw clearly what was happening in universities and government departments. Back then he was angry at his former comrades-in-arms for having traded their independence of thought for a position or contract. He gave free rein to his bitterness in a letter he wrote to his lawyers to thank them for defending him. In it he criticized other intellectuals for not having the courage of their convictions, for not having agreed to go to prison for their ideals, as he and others did.

"They will certainly suffer less as a result," he wrote. "But what about the dead? The dead are unable to defend themselves. Many of them intended to fight for China and her people, for truth and justice. I decided to take my chances to defend some of their points, even if I did not agree with all of them all the time. I know that my penalty was more serious because of all this action. But only by doing so can the dead rest in peace.... The trial has brought me a sort of relief and consolation. I once again have a clear conscience.... Yet what I am most concerned about is the loss of spirit and morality of our nation.... What I value is whether a human spirit has nobility — a noble and pure soul. In China, even intellectuals lack it."[5]

Almost twenty years later, the man seated across from me in a New York café does not seem bitter. Even though all of his former life has been lost, even though he spent more than four years in prison, even though he may never see China again in his lifetime, he remains optimistic. Yet Wang Juntao knows better than most that the future of China's political reforms will probably be at a standstill for a long time. He has just published a doctoral thesis at Columbia University dealing with the triumph of neo-conservatism in China. He knows that the conservative elements in the regime, at least for now, have the upper hand. It now seems possible for China to follow separate and apparently contradictory paths leading from the market economy and the monopoly of the Communist Party. He knows that Western premises relating to China's democratic evolution have been proven false. He knows Tiananmen Square's opportunity for democracy has not simply been postponed but that the country is experiencing an authoritarian change in policy that allows for no political reform. Chinese entrepreneurs who were supposed to demand a rule of law and launch China on the road to democratic reform have not only put up with the government's authoritarianism but also support it as party members. He knows as well that the village elections that were supposed to sow seeds of democracy in the Chinese countryside instead guaranteed the stronghold of Communist officials on local government. To invest in China, foreigners now have to go through an investment fund controlled by the son of former Premier Wen Jiabao. The few activists who still dare work toward reform in China opt to defend so-called citizens' rights, such as the right to clean water or education, rather than fundamental rights, such as freedom of speech, which are more likely to trigger repression from the authorities.

Wang Juntao knows that he and the other activists in exile who have not given up their fight may seem outdated, frozen like extinct species, in the amber of history. Despite all this, Wang Juntao says he remains confident. He still believes an enlightened leader will emerge who will open up China to democratic reform. I tell myself that the apparent detachment I detect in Wang Juntao is perhaps due to his new life as an academic. Toward the end of our meeting, the discussion becomes more disjointed. He tells me he remains in close contact with dissidents in China, thanks to the Internet. He explains how they avoid being censored by the authorities. We mention the upcoming hundredth anniversary of the fall of the last Chinese dynasty and the establishment of a democratic republic that only lasted a few months. I ask him if he finds it ironic that the father of this democratic experience, Sun Yat-sen, also found refuge in the United States. He concurs. This brings us to touch on the Chinese belief that history does not move in a straight line but repeats itself in a series of cycles, for Wang Juntao's struggle is the unfinished struggle he inherited from Sun Yat-sen and from all those who, in the course of the twentieth century, tried in vain to implant the idea of responsible government in China.

2

Sun Yat-sen's Unfinished Dream

Denver, Colorado, October 10, 1911

Sun Yat-sen, the man who would become the father of democracy in China, even the father of modern China, was raising money for his Revolutionary Alliance in the United States when the incident that would hasten the fall of the Qing Dynasty occurred in Hebei Province. A bomb exploded prematurely in a secret weapons factory run by young army cadets dedicated to overthrowing the dynastic regime.[1] The incident precipitated the revolt brewing in the Chinese army. Several generals defected and organized a rebellion. In less than two months, a majority of Chinese warlords united with the military rebels; the movement forced Emperor Puyi to abdicate. Sun Yat-sen was headed to Kansas City when news of the insurrection reached him. Usually he carried with him a deciphering apparatus that allowed him to read secret messages from his partisans in China. But that day he had forgotten the device. He learned from American newspapers that the moment he had been waiting for close to twenty years had finally arrived.[2] Sun Yat-sen could finally return home to work at establishing the Republic of China. Aware that the situation on the ground was still very fluid, he decided to first go through Europe to get the support of European governments. Without recognition from foreign countries, he knew that the Republican government would not be able to assert itself. In Shanghai, his partisans, who had worked secretly for years to undermine the imperial regime, saw him as a kind of saviour. China could finally become a democratic nation.

At first glance, Sun Yat-sen did not appear to be traditionally Chinese. He hated rice, wore a suit and tie, spoke English fluently, and had lived a good part of his life abroad. Yet he was definitely Chinese, a product of the China that, at the end of the nineteenth century, was emerging from its isolation and increasingly opening up to foreign influences. Sun Yat-sen was born into a peasant family near Canton in southern China in 1866. At a young age, he was taken in charge by one of his older brothers, who had become a prosperous merchant in Hawaii. This brother had Sun educated in missionary schools in Honolulu, which allowed him to be exposed to Christian values and democratic ideals. When he returned to China in 1883, Sun discovered a society crushed under the weight of the authoritarian government of the Qing. Sun Yat-sen saw in China a poor, superstitious society, ignorant of the modern ideas and technology prevalent in the West. Disappointed with his Chinese experience, Sun Yat-sen soon left for Hong Kong to study medicine. Yet his first ambition was to reform and modernize China, and he quickly abandoned medicine to dedicate himself full-time to this objective. One of the writings that most influenced him during his time in America was Abraham Lincoln's Gettysburg Address, in which Lincoln uttered the famous maxim of "government of the people, by the people, for the people." Lincoln's words, Sun would say later, served as the basis for his own political doctrine that he called "Three Principles of the People": nationalism, democracy, and the livelihood of the people.[3]

With his finely trimmed moustache, his business suits, and his conventional air, Sun Yat-sen looked more like a bourgeois revolutionary than a member of any resistance movement. When he began his political activities, he did not foresee revolution as a solution to China's problems. He first allied himself with reformers in the court who proposed transforming China into a constitutional monarchy. These attempts, however, were quelled by Dowager Empress Cixi, who had reigned as regent during the majority of the last twenty-five years of the Qing Dynasty. Seeing his reform proposals rejected by a large part of the intelligentsia, who did not consider him competent in the area because he had not studied the Chinese classics, Sun

Yat-sen concluded that peaceful reform was impossible. In 1894, he left for Hawaii, where he founded a society dedicated to abolishing the monarchy and establishing a democratic republic in China. He had to wait close to twenty years, living a life of exile that took him to Japan and Canada by way of Great Britain and the United States, where he travelled on a forged passport, before he could return to China to preside over the republic to which he had dedicated his life.

Sun Yat-sen represented, with others, the avant-garde of a new generation of Chinese drawn to democracy. The second half of the nineteenth century coincided with the golden age of the nation-state, a period of unprecedented intellectual ferment when European capitals were consumed with the ideas of the likes of Marx, Kant, and Montesquieu. Two key concepts of the time were freedom of the individual and democracy. More and more countries were establishing democratic parliamentary systems. These ideas reached young Chinese reformers through their travels, contacts with foreigners, or books that arrived aboard steamships in Shanghai. The development of a press with wide circulation gave rise to a number of newspapers and periodicals that helped spread ideas from abroad. The school of thought that emerged from contact with foreign ideas contended that China was not the centre of the world, as the mythology surrounding the Middle Kingdom had it, but a country among many others that could not develop at the same capacity as foreign powers unless it allowed its citizens to actively participate in public life. Inspired by this current, young Chinese intellectuals began studying and translating classics of Western philosophy.

One of the most famous was Liang Qichao, a young reformer who was the first to translate into Chinese Kant's concept of freedom. "Life and freedom are two essential elements that make man a man,"[4] wrote Liang. Since the Chinese cannot be considered free, he concluded, they are not yet "really men." To become "men," the Chinese must therefore acquire freedom of thought, freedom of speech, and the right to vote. If China hoped to be able to function in a more open and complex world, it had to abandon its dynastic regime and transform into a constitutional monarchy, a political system that notably allowed Great Britain to become one of the most powerful empires in history. One of the young Chinese strongly influenced by Liang's writings was Mao Zedong. The future revolutionary leader was still in school at that time. He boasted to his classmates that he knew by heart entire passages from the *New Citizen, a* magazine published by Liang. Later, following his conversion to communism, Mao denounced Liang Qichao and other reformers as "bourgeois democrats." Once in power, Mao banned Liang's writings.[5]

The Chinese reformers did not propose to overthrow the dynastic regime but to transform it. A number of them had studied in Japan, where they had seen close up the transformation of the Japanese imperial regime into a constitutional monarchy. The Japanese managed to import some of the West's best political and technological elements, including military know-how, which allowed them to inflict a humiliating defeat on China during the war of 1895. In the eyes of Liang and other Chinese thinkers, China needed to take on the methods and means of foreign powers, including the trappings of democracy, not to imitate them but to be in a better position to resist their economic, military, and even cultural assault. This nuance is key to understanding the role Chinese intellectuals played in the democratic reform movements of the twentieth century. Even if they believed China had to free itself from Confucian thought, they nevertheless continued to act, like Confucius, as advisers to the emperor and not as opponents to the government. Analysts such as Jean-Philippe Béja have wondered whether "this social group, which played a central role in bringing ideas of freedom and democracy to the public, was not at the same time an obstacle to the true democratization of society."[6] As we will see later, during the events of Tiananmen Square, many student leaders identified with the traditional role of the Chinese intellectual, which involved helping the regime fulfil its duties. The way they perceived their role was to prove detrimental in their dealings with the authorities during those fateful weeks in 1989.

At the beginning of the twentieth century, Imperial China was not any more inclined than later Chinese leaders to consider the change reformers proposed. For Empress Cixi, the idea of a constitutional monarchy where she would have to share power with an elected parliament was downright heretical. For more than two millennia, the dynastic regime had proved to be a remarkably durable form of government for China. The emperor's legitimacy stemmed from a mandate conferred by the gods. By virtue of this celestial mandate, the sovereign committed to provide for his subjects' needs. They, in exchange, vowed loyalty based on filial piety. The central administration was run by mandarins, the first true bureaucrats in history. Every year, the most promising graduates went to Beijing to take their imperial exams. The most talented had their names engraved on marble tablets in the gardens of the Confucius temple in Beijing. They were admitted to the privileged sanctuary of the mandarinate, where they devoted their lives to advising the emperor and seeing to the affairs of the empire. This meritocracy, with all the prestige and privilege it contained, had the advantage of ensuring that the emperor had the loyalty of the intelligentsia. The system was bonded by traditional values and the teachings of Confucius, which favoured loyalty and harmony. Confucian thought, recorded in the famous *Analects*, a series of precepts of life and rules of civic behaviour, served as a kind of state religion and political philosophy.

The sovereign's mandate, however, was not eternal. It could be revoked if he did not carry it out properly. The people, should the need arise, could legitimately overthrow the imperial regime under a right to rebellion. The gods would show their displeasure with the emperor, usually by a series of natural disasters, such as floods, droughts, earthquakes, or infestations of insects. While the "Mandate of Heaven" was deemed eternal, that of the regime that carried it out was not. Therein lies a fundamental difference with the concept of divine right on which most European monarchies were founded. Some historians believe the inherent conditions of the Mandate of Heaven contained "seeds of democracy"[7] or at the very least a rudimentary form of accountability of the sovereign to the people.

Starting in the 1850s, it was becoming obvious that this form of government was no longer appropriate for China. On one hand, the Qing leaders had a harder time containing the many popular uprisings spawned by the court's inability to respond to citizens' demands. The most bloody, the Taiping Rebellion, lasted about ten years and cost the lives of no fewer than twenty million people. The people's confidence in the Qing regime was also undermined by the government's increasing inability to counter the military, commercial, and technological threats from abroad. Two successive defeats against England during the Opium Wars were particularly humiliating for China. It only took a few days for the British navy to show its military superiority and to obtain from the Chinese significant concessions, such as the right to do business in the country's seaports, the handover of Hong Kong, and a ban on branding foreigners as barbarians in official documents, as was the custom at the court. The most humiliating incident for the Qing occurred in 1876, when a Franco-British expedition sent to Beijing to avenge the death of European nationals killed during riots in the coastal city of Tanjin met with so little resistance that the entire court had to flee the capital to one of its summer residences in Manchuria, on the other side of the Great Wall. To add insult to injury, French and British soldiers were able with complete impunity to set fire to the Summer Palace, one of the most sacred sites in Imperial China, before withdrawing with two bronzes statues. Today, these statues are still a source of contention between China and France. In 2009, they were auctioned in Paris by fashion designer Yves Saint Laurent's estate, despite protests by the Chinese authorities, who demanded their return to China.

In the face of China's repeated setbacks, what would be known as the "self-strengthening movement" emerged among intellectuals and aristocrats, warlords and entrepreneurs. Their goal was to adapt China to foreign science and technology in military and industrial matters to allow it to resist repeated assaults by European powers. The undisputed leader of this movement was Li Hongzhang, a former general, imposing in stature, who had helped quell the Taiping Rebellion. Over the years, Li modernized coal mining operations, built the country's first cotton mill, and established a rudimentary postal service as well as a telegraph network. Li was more of a modernizer, however, than a reformer with designs on the throne. His practical political philosophy was founded on the elementary principles of Confucius. The government's duties, he declared, quoting the *Analects*, were to ensure the means to defend itself, that the people had enough to eat, and to deserve the people's confidence.[8] He believed that foreign governments possessed these qualities and that this explained their superiority. Thanks to their leadership, military leaders of Li's quality became reformers, entrepreneurs, and administrators, and rebuilt a China left battered by a half-century of rebellion and confrontation with foreign armies. But their reconstruction work also revealed the failure of leadership of the Qing, who, entrenched in the Forbidden City in Beijing, were consumed by palace intrigues that undermined their authority and cut them off more each day from the people. This was probably the great paradox of the self-strengthening movement. In wanting to fortify China in the face of foreign threats, it exposed the weakness of the imperial regime for all to see.

At the end of the nineteenth century, the Qing Dynasty was divided between a conservative wing, led by Dowager Empress Cixi, and a reformative wing, led by the young Guangxu Emperor. Cixi, who had begun her life at court as a concubine, had managed to have her nephew installed on the throne and herself named regent. She was short, scarcely four-foot-eleven, an avid cigarette smoker, and a virtuoso at intrigue but ill-informed about life outside the Forbidden City. In 1898, shortly after having taken power, the child-emperor Guangxu, now an adult, decided to seek independence from his aunt. Realizing the regime needed to be modernized, and wrongly believing he would obtain Cixi's support, he launched a reform campaign that would be known as "the Hundred Days' Reform," which was the amount of time it took the empress to put an end to it. Guangxu was a man of the world. He read French and English newspapers, had the telephone installed in the Forbidden City, and abhorred the extravagances of the court and the role of the eunuchs, of whom he had bad childhood memories. The emperor was determined to give the court a new image and to modernize education, industry, the armed forces, and administration of the state. But before he could realize his plans, Empress Cixi had him arrested. She announced she would take back the reins of power. Guangxu had tried to harness the winds of change, but he obviously did not have his aunt's tactical skills. He was a frail man, in failing health and prone to depression. After an audience with him, an American diplomat described him as a young, smooth-cheeked man with a voice as "light and thin as a mosquito."[9] Some of the reformers who had joined the Guangxu's campaign were executed. Others, such as Liang Qichao, the translator of Kant and the first to exalt individual freedom, managed to escape to Hong Kong. China, not for the only time in its history, had missed an opportunity for reform.

Cixi's coup d'état did not strengthen the legitimacy of the court or improve the running of the government, and it certainly did not dash hopes for reform. It only exacerbated problems. Faced with the government's growing inertia, several groups began to substitute themselves for authorities in providing public services, beginning with study societies that came into being in Shanghai. These organizations arose from necessity more than from some sort of thirst for political action. They were citizens' groups willing to offer public services such as health care and education, which the local governments appeared increasingly incapable of providing. Shortly after, chambers of commerce appeared, set up to defend the interests of Chinese tradesmen in their relationships with foreigners; this created a second power centre independent from the Chinese state. Gradually, inexorably, the imperial regime was losing its hold over Chinese society.

At the turn of the century, China had become a political tower of Babel: intellectuals who dreamed of democracy and reform, Chinese business people who lived Western lifestyles in the merchant neighbourhoods of Shanghai and Canton, warlords fighting over the countryside, and a population that bore the brunt of this anarchy and of the imperial power's inability to meet its basic needs.

Isolated in her apartments in the Forbidden City, Empress Cixi failed to understand the centrifugal forces threatening the survival of the court and was at a loss to fend them off. It is in this fertile ground for instability that the Boxer Rebellion in 1900 was about to deal the regime its final blow.

The Boxer Rebellion was essentially a revolt against the intrusive presence of foreigners in China. It began with the massacre of forty-eight Catholic missionaries in the provincial capital of Taiyuan before spreading to Beijing, where rebels besieged foreign embassies. The Boxers believed they had supernatural powers, including immunity from gunfire. Rather than quell the rebellion, Empress Cixi gave it her tacit approval. The siege of the embassies lasted close to two months until an expeditionary force of eight countries arrived that would crush the revolt. The Qing were forced to sign another humiliating treaty that required them to pay more than $300 million in compensation to foreign powers.

Discredited by the Boxer fiasco, weakened by the foreign occupation of Beijing, Cixi came to the conclusion in 1901 that the only way to save the imperial regime was to open the door to the democratic reforms she had always opposed. Her "new policies" program allowed for a nine-year transition toward a new constitutional monarchy. Meanwhile, the establishment of elected provincial parliaments would serve to prepare the ground for a national election. The Qing thus hoped to consolidate their power in the regions. But the provincial parliaments ended up becoming centres of opposition to the court. Empress Cixi died in 1908, along with her plans for reform. She was buried in a magnificent tomb, surrounded by an impressive supply of her favourite cigarettes. The imperial regime did not survive long after the death of the empress. On January 12, 1912, the young Emperor Puyi, only six years old, abdicated. After more than two hundred years, the Qing Dynasty toppled like an aging tree. There was no real revolution or war of independence; the most respected general at the court, Yuan Shikai, had the child-emperor's mother sign a formal surrender, guaranteeing them both a generous pension and permission to continue living in the Forbidden City.

To replace the imperial regime, the text of surrender announced nothing less than the establishment of a "perfect government." Yet beyond the will to modernize the state and rid China of the Qing, who at the end of their regime were facing a powerful nationalist backlash against their Manchu origins, there was no consensus among reformers about what form the new government should take. Above all, there was no leader who could rally the forces of change behind a constitutional project. Sun Yat-sen, the man who came closest to this role, was recognized as the nominal leader of the Revolutionary Alliance, which included most of the groups dedicated to abolishing the Qing Dynasty. Yet he had lived abroad for the past twenty years. His partisans had taken part in some unsuccessful attempts at armed insurrection in the south of the country, but Sun himself mostly owed his notoriety to a much publicized incident in which Qing agents had abducted him and held him prisoner inside the Chinese embassy in London in 1896. He had managed to slip a note to one of his friends, who alerted the press and the British government. A judge then ordered him freed in accordance with the principle of habeas corpus. The news had spread to China, where it provided Sun Yat-sen with instant fame.

When Sun arrived in Shanghai by steamboat barely a month before Emperor Puyi's abdication, in December 1911, General Yuan Shikai was already recognized as the leader of the Republican forces. A provisional parliament set up in the former capital of Nanjing nevertheless elected Sun Yat-sen president of the burgeoning republic. Aware that General Yuan alone was capable of uniting the disparate forces of the reform movement, Sun Yat-sen soon resigned from his position as president to offer it to the military leader. It was deemed necessary to quickly elect a national parliament that could give China a constitution on which the young republic would be built. Having transformed his revolutionary movement into a powerful electoral machine, the Kuomintang, Sun Yat-sen easily came out the big winner in the election. But the success was also due to the political brilliance of his assistant party leader, Song Jiaoren. Only thirty years old, he was said to be pedantic and arrogant, two major faults in a country that valued wisdom and humility in its leaders. Nevertheless, he proved a clever politician, and his message resonated with the Chinese, at least the forty million who had the right to vote, scarcely 10 per cent of the population. This, the country's first democratic exercise, was actually limited to men older than twenty-one years of age who had an elementary school diploma and held property worth at least $500 or who paid taxes of $2 or more. The electoral law prohibited the illiterate, opium smokers, people who were bankrupt or not deemed of sound mind, and women.

Imperfect as it was, this first national democratic poll heralded a new political era for China. It was short-lived, however. The ideal of the republic was to vanish in a pool of blood on the platform of the Shanghai train station, even before the new parliament had a chance to sit. On March 20, 1913, Song Jiaoren, like other members of parliament, was heading to Beijing for the first session of the legislature. He was expected to be chosen prime minister. But even before he could board the train, a man armed with a pistol intercepted him and shot him twice point-blank. Taken to hospital, Song Jiaoren died two days later. General Yuan Shikai, making the most of the crisis, seized power. He was actually suspected of having ordered Song's assassination. But nothing was ever proven, as the suspects in the assassination attempt disappeared under mysterious circumstances before they could be tried. The doctors would later say they had been ordered to wait for Yuan's authorization before treating Song Jiaoren's wounds. The authorization never came. China's democratic spring did not last long. As for the murder of Song Jiaoren, its repercussions were symbolically as important to China as the assassination of the Archduke of Austria a year later in Sarajevo was for Europe. That incident triggered the First World War. Had Song not been assassinated, China would have been on the way to becoming the first democratic republic in Southeast Asia. Instead, it sank into militarism and division.

General Yuan Shikai did not burden himself with the trappings of the republic for long. In order to eliminate the main centre of opposition to his authoritarian ambitions, he outlawed Sun Yat-sen's party, the Kuomintang, which held a majority of seats in parliament. Then he intimidated or bribed the remaining elected members. In 1914, Yuan finally abolished parliament and adopted a new constitution, granting him nearly absolute power as well as presidency for life. Parliament, in his opinion, was not functional. Of its eight hundred members, he told people close to him, only two hundred were competent, two hundred were passive, and the rest useless. To establish his authority, Yuan censored the press, pursued his opponents, and restored the worship of Confucius, discredited since the fall of the Qing. The following year, unable to resist the temptation of absolutism, he had himself crowned emperor, putting on airs of a Chinese Napoleon. His coronation ceremony took place at the Temple of Heaven in Beijing. Fearing an assassination attempt, Yuan had himself driven in an armoured car. Once there, dressed in a traditional purple tunic embroidered with dragons, he gave himself the name Hongxian, meaning "constitutional abundance."[10] It's uncertain if in doing so Yuan revealed an acute sense of irony or if he hoped to confer some sort of democratic legitimacy on his self-proclaimed reign. His title nevertheless reveals how much the Republican vocabulary was now part of the Chinese political discourse, even if it remained meaningless. In any case, Yuan's reign was to be short-lived. Pressured from all sides, he agreed to abolish the monarchy scarcely two months after being crowned. He died the following year of a blood infection, in ridicule and disgrace. Far from solidifying the base of the burgeoning republic, Yuan had destroyed its foundation. Barely four years after the fall of the Qing, China had fallen back into anarchy and division. By wanting to centralize the power for himself, the old general had inadvertently delivered the country to the warlords.

During the general's reign, no fewer than seven provinces declared their independence from the central government. They were ruled by military leaders who ran their territories rather like the kings of medieval Europe. The Beijing government's only legitimacy came from diplomatic recognition and from the fact that it still controlled the country's customs revenues. Between 1916 and 1928, China had twenty-six prime ministers and nine heads of state, each one weaker and less powerful than the next. Otherwise, the country's stability was maintained by an uneasy balance of power between regional governors, eccentric warlords who distinguished themselves by their lifestyles as much as their political philosophies. The leader from Shandong province, General Zhang Zongchang, was known for his extreme violence and for his harem of concubines, which included Chinese, French, and Russian mistresses, as well as one American. He proclaimed himself "Great General of Justice and Might." Feng Yuxiang, called the "Christian General," converted to Methodism, married a YMCA employee, and had his troops sing Christmas carols. Wu Peifu, the warlord of Hunan, was considered the most educated of the warlords. Nicknamed the "Philosopher General," he was fond of Chinese calligraphy and hung a portrait of George Washington on his office wall. No doubt the most avant-garde of the military leaders was Yan Xishan, from Shanxi. Nicknamed the "Model Governor," he tried to modernize his province by developing the coal and steel industries, encouraged irrigation, and forbade his subjects to bind women's feet. He claimed that his political philosophy consisted of nothing less than militarism, nationalism, anarchism, democracy, capitalism, communism, individualism, imperialism, universalism, and paternalism.[11] Such eclecticism reveals how China, only a few years after its revolution, was in a state of anarchy and dysfunction as acute as in the last years of the Qing Dynasty. Moreover, it reveals how much its plans for a republic had become a parody.

Despite many personal and political setbacks during these years of turbulence, Sun Yat-sen never gave up on his democratic ideals. After yielding the presidency to General Yuan for the good of the country, he agreed to sit in his government as minister of railways. When General Yuan declared Sun Yat-sen's party, the Kuomintang, illegal, Sun realized he had to leave the country as soon as possible. He took refuge in Japan, where he founded a new revolutionary alliance, the KMT, and where he set about refining his political plans, which essentially aimed at overthrowing Beijing's puppet government. The building of the republic, it seemed, was destined to be started over and over again.

In 1922, Sun Yat-sen secretly arrived in Canton in the south of China, where he intended to establish a regional government that would serve as a springboard for his taking control of the entire country. Chiang Kai-shek, his young military assistant, soon joined him. Not having the financial or military resources to see the operation through, Sun did not shun joining forces with Chinese Communists and accepted the assistance of Soviet military advisers. He also asked the United States and European powers to form an expeditionary force to overthrow the Beijing government and bring him to power, a request they would decline. Nevertheless, with the help of Communist sympathizers and Soviet advisers, Sun and Chiang managed to establish a provisional government in Canton. Sun's administration, however, would mostly become known for its inefficiency, which confirms that the father of Chinese democracy was more of a theorist than an accomplished practitioner of government. Meanwhile, China sank deeper and deeper into banditry. Warlords fought over the income from the opium trade and taxed people with impunity while armed gangs wandered the countryside, terrorizing villages and making kidnapping a lucrative industry.

Gradually, Sun Yat-sen came to the conclusion that China was not ready for democracy. Sun now believed that there were three stages to go through before arriving at a democratically elected government. As soon as they took power, after overthrowing the Beijing government, Sun's revolutionary party would put the country under military trusteeship. This would be followed by a period in which the people would be educated in democracy. When the people were deemed ready to exercise the right to vote, the revolutionary government would organize an election and China would become a real republic. Sun, however, did not know how long each of the phases would last. In 1924, two years after establishing his base in Canton, aware he did not have long to live, Sun travelled secretly to Beijing in the hope of negotiating a truce with the regime. He died there of liver cancer a few months later. It is indicative of the leader's complexity that Sun was given two funerals, one Christian, the other Chinese. Stalin even sent a used coffin from Moscow for Sun's burial. His family, declining Stalin's offer, buried him in a grave outside Beijing.

Sun, the spiritual leader of the Chinese democratic movement, would become an even stronger source of inspiration for the country's reformers after his death. In churches, his supporters replaced crucifixes with his portrait, and his name adorned the packages of one of China's most popular brands of cigarettes. After a hard campaign, his military right-hand man, Chiang Kai-shek, managed to unify forces in the south and seize Beijing in 1928. One of Chiang's first actions was to visit Sun Yat-sen's grave. Chiang seemed determined to establish, if not a democratic government, at the very least a government of national unity to which the Chinese could rally. To mark the beginning of a new political era, Chiang had the capital moved from Beijing to Nanjing. In 1929, a special conference of the Nationalist Party decreed the party would form a trusteeship government until 1935, long enough to educate the Chinese in the ways of democracy. Chiang vowed to follow his mentor Sun Yat-sen's political plan to move toward democracy and concluded that his own legitimacy and his government's involved worshipping Sun. Chiang had Sun's remains transferred to a magnificent mausoleum on a hill near Nanjing. It became mandatory to salute Sun's portrait and read some of his political writings in public meetings. These also appeared in textbooks.

To consolidate his government, Chiang appointed several warlords to ministerial positions. He also appointed a number of foreign advisers, including automobile magnate Henry Ford, although Ford only agreed to advise Chiang providing he did not have to travel to China. Despite the Nationalists' victory, the country still remained dangerously unstable and divided; several governors in the regions only outwardly professed support of the new government. Out of instinct or necessity, Chiang Kai-shek gradually abandoned his democratic ambitions and withdrew into more familiar territory: authoritarianism. After all, he was a professional soldier who had led the famous Whampoa Military Academy in Canton, the same one that introduced Western military techniques to China. Several of his graduates followed Chiang to Nanjing and were part of his entourage.

Chiang intended to impose strict military discipline on his government, even on the country. He launched the New Life Movement, a code of conduct that valued Confucian principles of filial piety and social harmony and banned spitting or smoking in public. Yet Chiang Kai-shek's paternalism quickly took on overtones of fascism. He proclaimed himself Generalissimo and led the government with an iron hand with the help of a secret police force and a personal guard dressed with blue shirts, a dress code that would later reappear with the followers of Mussolini. Chiang was convinced that China was sinking into moral decline. He criticized intellectuals for undermining the country's traditional values, especially those associated with the May Fourth Movement. That movement arose from demonstrations in Tiananmen Square against the humiliating treatment of China at the Versailles Conference in 1919, where the treaty ending the First World War was negotiated. The intellectuals of the May Fourth Movement believed China had to open up more to the world. In doing so they took up the torch of the self-strengthening movement of the end of the nineteenth century. One of their popular slogans was that China must make way for the two gentlemen of reform: "Mr. Science and Mr. Democracy: Only these two could save China from the political, moral, academic and intellectual darkness in which it finds itself."[12] Their example would serve later as an inspiration for the student movement of 1989.

The May Fourth Movement was less of a political movement, however, than a philosophical cri du coeur. Its leaders may have despaired at China's state of paralysis but had no program or strategy to introduce Chinese society to liberal democracy. Their desire for a rapprochement between Chinese and Western philosophy did produce peculiar meetings, such as American philosopher John Dewey's two-year stay in China, where he lectured widely. The leaders of the movement had a difficult time gaining a political foothold in a political landscape where warlords overshadowed a weak parliament. From the mid-1920s on, they were certainly no match for Chiang Kai-shek's authoritarianism. With the outbreak of the war against Japan, many intellectuals associated with the May Fourth Movement simply faded away. Some agreed out of patriotic duty to serve in the Kuomintang regime; others joined Mao in the resistance movement.

To muzzle the opposition, which was growing increasingly strong in the face of his authoritarian methods, Chiang censored the press and ordered writers and artists to produce works celebrating the virtues of Chinese civilization. Far from evolving into a democrat, Chiang Kai-shek was behaving more and more like a dictator. In 1936, the year he had promised to establish democracy, he proclaimed instead his infallibility with his famous declaration: "I am the Generalissimo, I do not err. China cannot do well without me."[13]

Twenty-five years after the fall of the Qing, China had missed its attempt at democracy. The Chinese would now be subjected to ten years of war against Japan and fifteen years of civil war between Chiang Kai-shek's Nationalists and Mao's Communists. These two conflicts unfolded simultaneously and left the country depleted, its population exhausted. The failure of the republic had serious repercussions for China. It substantiated the theory, still widespread today, that liberal democracy is incompatible with China, as if the country lacked a gene allowing it to govern itself with an elected parliament. In 1912, conditions were not favourable for China to succeed in moving toward democracy. The imperial regime had fallen almost too quickly, before reformers had time to organize a smooth transition. Not only had the country been unable to take its first steps toward democracy, despite establishing regional parliaments and town councils, but China did not have the necessary institutions for making its republic successful, starting with a rule of law. Since a large part of the country was in the hands of the warlords, military commanders emerged as leaders of the Republican movement. The natural sympathies of Yuan Shikai, the old general who would be known as the saboteur of the republic, led him to lean more toward authoritarianism than parliamentarianism. It was not without reason that Sun Yat-sen concluded the Chinese were not ready for democracy, that they needed time to learn it under the supervision of a military government before being able to responsibly and effectively choose their leaders. China, however, fell back into authoritarianism before it could benefit from an incubatory period that could have given its democracy time to become viable.

The corollary of this reasoning is that China can only be governed by an authoritarian single-party regime. Today still, leaders of the Communist Party constantly postpone the date of China's democratization on the pretext that China is not developed enough to elect its government. The arguments are well known: the Chinese are too poor, not educated enough; the country is too large for a liberal democracy to work there. This becomes both a mental block for many Chinese and a way of justifying a single-party regime.

China's early failure in democratic experimentation has stigmatized the Chinese political discourse in another way. Each authoritarian Chinese leader in the twentieth century has felt the need to sing the praises of democracy even though his actions were steeped in authoritarianism. Chiang Kai-shek, as a disciple of Sun Yat-sen, declared himself a democrat but deemed he had to impose an authoritarian regime before the people could be entitled to exercise their right to vote. Mao, in launching the Communist Revolution, spoke of instituting "true democracy," even if terror and political repression reached new heights under his reign. From Deng Xiaoping to Hu Jintao, the Communist leaders who succeeded Mao made a distinction between democracy within the Communist Party and Western "bourgeois democracy," which they claimed was not compatible with the character of the Chinese people. Such discourse has allowed them to justify the monopoly of power exercised by the Communist Party, reject liberal democracy as being unsuitable to Chinese reality, and counter accusations of authoritarianism levelled both inside and outside China. Paradoxically, democracy, or rather the justification of its absence, from then on became an integral part of Chinese political discourse. Despite its failure, Sun Yat-sen's democratic dream, through its unfulfilled promise, continues to inhabit the Chinese political universe.

3
Mao's Democracy

Sensing the end of the war against the Japanese was drawing near and anticipating the decisive battle against Chiang Kai-shek's Nationalists, Mao convened the Seventh Congress of the Communist Party to lay the foundation for the Chinese state as he saw it. The previous congress had been held seventeen years before, in Moscow. At the time, Chinese Communists were on the run, pursued by Chiang Kai-shek's Nationalist armies. The context of the seventh congress was quite different. Mao's armies now had momentum, and discussion among Communists centred on what to do when they finally took power. Many of them had survived the Long March and had fought alongside Mao for years. This seventh congress, held in Yan'an Province, the base of Communist forces, would confirm Mao as the movement's supreme leader and adopt his thinking as its guiding principles.

As he addressed his comrades-in-arms, Mao spoke of the need to wipe out the Kuomintang dictatorship. But he also vowed to replace it with a fundamentally democratic regime. "We must carry out democratic reform throughout the country," declared Mao to members of the Communist congress. "The people's right to freedom of expression and free press, the right to assemble, to organize, freedom of thought, and belief in the freedom to make choices about one's own body are the most important freedoms." Mao's iteration would soon seem unrecognizable to most Chinese, but the end justified the means. Mao's call for democracy was meant to gain the support of a majority of Chinese. That is why he called for a coalition government that would include several parties other than the Communist Party. But in Mao's mind, such an alliance could only be temporary and one of convenience. Once in power, he intended the Communist Party to exercise absolute rule in the realization of its socialist revolution. It would be, to use the expression of sinologist Michel Bonnin, "democracy in the service of dictatorship."[1]

When we examine Mao's totalitarian body of work, it is natural to conclude that the ideal of democracy in China disappeared into a political black hole once the Communists came to power in 1949 and only emerged from this abyss after the death of the Great Helmsman at the end of the 1970s. Yet Mao's reign of terror over China, which lasted for more than a quarter-century, overshadowed a complex relationship the Communist leader had with the idea of democracy from the time he planned his revolution in the Chinese countryside. An examination of Mao's writings and declarations from the 1920s through to the Cultural Revolution shows that in his lifetime the Communist leader juggled with no fewer than half a dozen definitions of democracy. He spoke in turn of party democracy, democratic centralism, democracy of the people, democratic dictatorship, real democracy, and finally great democracy. All these concepts and slogans served to legitimize his Communist Revolution and reinforce his hold on power. This did not make Mao a democrat; on the contrary, he and his Communist successors, over the course of decades, have moulded, stretched, modified, and twisted the notion of democracy to adapt it to the Communist agenda that today still influences the way democracy is viewed in China. It informs the chronic misunderstanding between the West and the Chinese regime on the need and the nature of political reform in China.

Contrary to other Communist leaders in Asia, including his alter ego Zhou Enlai, Mao did not learn the principles of Marxism in the faculties or capitals of Europe. His intellectual training took place in clandestine Communist groups in the south of China. As such, Mao's political thought was constantly conditioned by tactical considerations. Mao first invoked democracy to unify Communist forces and gain the support of rural populations when he was fighting Nationalist armies in the late 1920's. After a first defeat against Chiang Kai-shek in 1927, the Communists had taken refuge in the mountains of Hunan and Yunan in the southwest of China. That was when Mao declared the Party had to be like a fish in water. It had to take inspiration from the people's ideas, adapt them to the Marxist doctrine then reintroduce them in the population where they would be transformed into action. This was largely a one-way relationship since people didn't really have a say in the operation. Mao, in fact, relied on Lenin's principle of "democratic centralism," whereby the Party is sovereign in guiding the people toward the realization of socialism. In reality, this conception of democracy through the party was not much more than a slogan, since Mao and the Red Army at the time were beating a retreat from Nationalist forces that besieged them in the mountains. Indeed, in the 1930s, Mao's life was mostly that of a guerrilla leader. The Communists were preparing to undertake their Long March, a superhuman ordeal that would cost the majority of them their lives but would establish the myth of their tenacity. For the time being, the march would take them far away from the centre of power in Beijing.

Despite his profession of democratic faith, Mao at the time was already indulging in one of the Great Purges that would become his trademark, his method of eliminating people he deemed ideologically impure or potential rivals to his leadership. In 1931, Mao allied himself with the Communist base in Jiangxi, and their combined forces inflicted a rare defeat on Nationalists at the Battle of Changsha. The soldiers had scarcely begun to savour victory when Mao convened a special meeting of the party to purge it of its anti-revolutionary elements. He accused leaders of the Jiangxi base of being elitists allied with the landowners and rich peasants and ordered them liquidated. When the massacre and torture were over, the number of officers and soldiers executed by firing squad was estimated in the tens of thousands. According to Mao, the Communist Party perhaps had to listen to the people and practise democracy in its armies, but he himself firmly intended to exercise total control over the party and violently eliminate any opponent he deemed a threat. Nor would he be inclined to tolerate any dissidence whatsoever.

In 1942, in the midst of civil war against the Nationalists and at the height of the resistance against the Japanese, Mao launched the first of several "rectification movements." Many young Chinese intellectuals, whose democratic aspirations were blocked by the Nationalists, had joined Mao in the Yan'an liberated area. Most of them were from wealthy families in coastal cities where they were used to speaking their mind. Many of these young intellectuals were convinced that the Communist zone offered more freedom than Nationalist regions and naively believed they could criticize the privileges of Communist officials. They quickly became disillusioned when they realized that democratic freedom according to Mao was only a slogan, that freedom of expression in the "red" Communist zones was even less tolerated than in Chiang Kai-shek's "white" zones. Mao, feeling his authority challenged by these young bourgeois who, in addition, behaved as though they were superior to the peasants, sent hundreds of them to the countryside to be re-educated.

At the time, Mao and the other Chinese Communist leaders widely shared Marx and Lenin's vision of democracy. Essentially, for Marxist Leninists, liberal democracy, as it exists in capitalist countries such as France, Great Britain, and the United States, was only another instrument for oppressing the working class. It was a false democracy, as the political system was dominated by capitalist owners; by exercising their right to vote, workers basically legitimized those who exploited them. All they got to choose, as it were, was their oppressor. Real democracy, the only one that could respond to the aspirations of the people, was the brand of democracy practised through the Communist Party from the moment the proletarian revolution was achieved. This "democratic centralism," conceived by Mao, worked more or less as follows: a question was discussed inside the party, which made a decision that would then be implemented. The party agreed to consult broadly before convincing people to accept the decision it had made.

For Mao, the difficulty was that the Communist Revolution had been envisioned by Marx to apply to industrialized societies, not agrarian societies such as China. In China there was no working class large enough to rebel against the capitalist class. In 1929, scarcely 3 per cent of the members of the Chinese Communist Party came from the proletariat. Therefore, the Marxist doctrine had to be adapted to Chinese reality. Mao concluded that the Chinese, before being ready for a socialist democracy, first had to experience liberal democracy, which they would reject rather quickly, before finally embracing socialism. Marxist-Leninist doctrine does provides for going through a bourgeois revolution before arriving at a socialist revolution, as if workers first have to become aware of their exploitation before being able to rebel. There were precedents for this kind of doctrinal compromise in the large Marxist family. Lenin himself, shortly after the Bolshevik Revolution, came to the conclusion that Russians were not ready for the Communist economy. For several years he had to call on industrial capitalists to rescue the Soviet economy from collapse and establish a transition period between capitalism and communism. From the 1940s on, Mao came to the conclusion that China needed the same kind of political transition, that the country had to experience liberal democracy as a transition to socialist democracy.

Mao, as opposed to Marx, did not have the luxury of putting the finishing touches on his political philosophy in the calm and comfort of the London Library, where the father of Marxism spent much of his time. During the approximately fifteen years between the beginning of the Long March and the Communist victory, Mao carried his revolutionary ideas in a political knapsack, constantly adapting his strategies to an unstable, changing political landscape. His revolution took a long and tortuous route, forcing him to forge alliances and make ideological detours that, in other circumstances, would have seemed to defy the laws of logic and gravity.

When Mao emerged from the Long March in the fall of 1935, after a nightmarish crossing of the Tibetan Plateau in the middle of winter, he had lost 90 per cent of his army; he was even reduced to living in a cave in Shaanxi, a sandy plateau in the centre of China. Few would have thought he could survive. But history came to his rescue. Before Chiang Kai-shek had the chance to begin a final offensive against the Communists, the Japanese launched an attack on China. Suddenly, the Nationalists had to fight on two fronts: against the Japanese to the east and against the Communists to the north and west. Even if the Japanese invasion favoured Mao, inasmuch as it weakened Chiang Kai-shek's Nationalists, a Japanese victory would be the worst scenario for his Communist Revolution. Paradoxically, China's only hope of beating the Japanese lay in a coalition of Nationalists and Communists. Moscow and Washington, which also feared a Japanese victory, put pressure on Chiang Kai-shek and Mao to unite. Chiang resisted, dithering. He felt that with enough help from the Americans he could overcome the Japanese armies. However, his position was precarious. Faced with the advance of the Japanese, he had to move the capital, his government, and a large part of the country's heavy industry to the city of Chongqing, on the Yangtze, far from the country's coast and out of reach of the Japanese. Chiang's stubbornness frustrated his main American adviser, General Joseph "Vinegar" Stillwell, who was dispatched to China to co-ordinate the resistance against Japan. Stillwell served as military attaché in China and spoke Chinese. He had only contempt for Chiang, whom he described as "ignorant, illiterate, superstitious peasant son of a bitch."[2]

The forced alliance between Nationalists and Communists was finally made possible by the incredible kidnapping of Chiang Kai-shek in December 1936. Chiang had gone to see one of his generals, Yang Hucheng, in the city of X'ian. It was a trap, for Yang had secretly allied himself with the Communists. In the early hours of the morning, he had Chiang arrested. Chiang tried to flee in his nightshirt, without his dentures, which remained on the night table. Mao, delighted by this turn of events, wanted to have Chiang, his sworn enemy, executed. But Moscow intervened and forced the two men to discuss an alliance. Stalin was convinced Chiang was in a better position than Mao to prevent the Japanese from conquering China. Mao complied and Zhou Enlai was dispatched to X'ian to negotiate with Chiang. The two men agreed to a truce in order to fight the Japanese, and the Generalissimo was set free.

The alliance of the Nationalists and the Communists, who fought on different fronts and not side by side, helped slow the advance of the Japanese. The truce also gave the Communists time to replenish their forces without fearing the attacks of Chiang Kai-shek. This alliance, which lasted until the end of the war in 1945, led to a complex and intense political ballet between

Washington, Moscow, Chiang Kai-shek, and Mao. It was a period in which Mao praised the merits of democracy to draw support both from the Chinese population and the Americans. For even if they were allies of convenience in a fight to the finish against Japan, Chiang and Mao never lost sight of the fundamental objective of their struggle: power in what would be China once the war ended.

The idea of an alliance between the Communists and the Nationalists was not new. As early as 1936, Mao had proposed to Chiang that together they establish a unified democratic republic of all China. At the time, Mao was refining his political doctrine in a series of writings. According to his logic, the democratic dictatorship that was supposed to unify all classes was only provisional.[3] Its objective was to free China of the imperialists and those whom he called the "reactionary traitors." Mao called this government the "new democracy," a bourgeois democratic revolution led by several political parties. According to Mao, this bourgeois revolution should only serve as a prelude to a socialist revolution. In actual fact, Mao's proposal didn't go anywhere. It was ultimately a theoretical exercise with no concrete possibilities, as the country was at war. But it had the advantage of allowing Mao to show Chinese intellectuals wary of Chiang Kai-shek's authoritarianism and the American government that he was committed to patriotism and democracy.

Mao's American contact in China was John Service, one of four career diplomats who would be known as the China Hands and long criticized in the United States for having lost China to the Communists. In 1943, Service, with the help of a dozen soldiers, established a base near Yenan, close to Mao's headquarters. The Americans nicknamed their base "Dixie Mission" because it was in rebel territory.[4] Mao and his Communist staff often went to see Service at the Dixie Mission, where the American diplomat treated the future Great Helmsman to movies and even dances. The Americans may have been reduced to living in caves dug into hillsides with no running water, but they weren't ones to deny themselves a bit of entertainment. During his discussions with Mao, Service came to the conclusion that the

Communist leader was a democrat. Mao did nothing to discourage this impression. "All the American soldiers who fight in China," he said to Service, "must be living advertisements for democracy; they must speak of democracy to all the Chinese they meet."[5] Mao claimed he was in favour of establishing a constitutional government in which members of parliament were freely elected by the people. He even proposed to meet President Roosevelt to convince him to abandon his support of Chiang Kai-shek. Most likely that was the real goal of his charm offensive on John Service. Apparently this was successful, as Service recommended to Roosevelt that he drop Chiang Kai-shek's Nationalists and support Mao. The president, however, did not share Service's view of Mao, and he did not follow through on his emissary's recommendation.

In Washington, Roosevelt had come to the conclusion, despite or perhaps because of Mao's democratic rhetoric, that Mao was not a real Communist but rather a leader of an agrarian socialist movement. The Americans were convinced that as soon as the war was over they could convince Mao to join the Nationalists in a democratic type of national government. Hadn't Mao himself already proposed as much? Above all, Roosevelt hoped to prevent China from sinking into civil war once the Japanese were defeated. In November 1944, the new American ambassador to China, Patrick Hurley, a former cowboy turned politician, went to see Mao with the intention of forging a political pact between Communists and Nationalists. Mao set out his conditions: a coalition government, a joint military council, American supplies, and the release of political prisoners. Hurley had an official document drafted containing Mao's requests but added to it the notions of democracy and freedom. Mao signed it without hesitation.

It was not until August 1945, two weeks before the Japanese surrender, that real negotiations began on forming a coalition government between Nationalists and Communists. Patrick Hurley went personally to fetch Mao by plane to bring him to Chongqing for a constitutional conference. Twenty years after the start of their armed conflict, Mao and Chiang Kai-shek were finally to meet face to face, ostensibly to share power in a liberated China.

But it was too much to ask of these sworn enemies. During the first days of the conference, Mao and Chiang gave the impression they wanted to collaborate. Mao even proposed a toast at an official dinner, declaring "Long live President Chiang Kai-shek!"[6] Behind the scenes, however, the two men outdid each other in tactics to scuttle discussions, each one making demands the other could not accept. The Americans and the Soviets, however, were adamant about a coalition government. Despite the appearance of an agreement, the fighting between Nationalist and Communist forces would soon resume with even more intensity. It would only end with the victory of the Communists in 1949.

On October 1, 1949, Mao proclaimed the founding of the People's Republic of China from atop the Forbidden City in Beijing. Chiang Kai-shek was still on the run in Sichuan, from where he and what remained of his government would end up reaching Taiwan. Faithful to his plan, Mao announced that his first government would be a "bourgeois" type democracy, made up of several parties and classes, some of which were destined to disappear. The previous month, in September 1949, Mao had called a consultative conference made up of representatives from several political leanings. The common program adopted by this conference was a model of human rights and democracy. It proclaimed the primacy of rights for the Chinese, particularly freedom of thought, speech, publication, assembly, association, correspondence, and movement, as well as personal freedom, the choice of one's place of residence, religion, and the right to demonstrate. It guaranteed property rights and ensured that the people's representatives would be elected via universal suffrage.[7] The one exception was "political reactionaries," who were deprived of these rights: the category rather quickly allowed Mao to crush all those who opposed his will or didn't share his opinions.

Despite their victory, the Communists still did not enjoy widespread support from the population. To obtain it, Mao gave the new republic all the trappings of democracy and reconciliation. One of the leaders of the Democratic League, who had been persecuted by Chiang Kai-shek, was appointed vice-mayor of Beijing. General Fu, the Nationalist military leader who changed sides and delivered the capital to the Communists, was appointed to the cabinet. Mao even called Mrs. Sun Yat-sen to his side, put her up in a villa, and appointed her as one the regime's six vice-presidents. Like the Nationalists twenty years earlier, the Communists used worship of Sun Yat-sen to reinforce their support in the population. Yet it was not the father of modern China's democratic ideal they used for propaganda purposes, but his past as a revolutionary who contributed to the fall of the Qing autocratic regime. In private, Mao's entourage described these non-Communists as decorative vases. Mao himself left little doubt as to his true intentions when he said that this "new democracy" was really a "joint dictatorship of the revolutionary classes." At this embryonic stage of the People's Republic, however, the Communists still needed capitalist entre-preneurs to make the economy work as a transition to a planned socialist economy. The number-two man in the regime, Liu Shaoqi, declared with some ingenuity that the new China had to tolerate a degree of "capitalist exploitation," that eliminating the bourgeoisie too quickly would result in the failure of industries that China needed. He added it would probably be necessary to let the bourgeoisie exist and even develop for several decades. The Communists' objective was to gradually nationalize the large industrial groups.

Nevertheless, Chinese Communist leaders couldn't be seen to be too soft on the country's capitalists. In 1951, the regime launched a first "recti-fication" campaign in which peasants were encouraged to hold public trials of those who were accused of exploiting them. Wealthy people and landowners were marched onto platforms and forced to confess their crimes before being beaten and often put to death. The minister of public security even published a manual explaining how to hold an accusation meeting. Children were encouraged to denounce their parents, workers to denounce their colleagues, and neighbours to mutually denounce one another. Officially the goal of the rectification campaign was to put the finishing touches on the class struggle, but it was also a pretext for a wave of paranoia and settling of scores in neighbourhoods, villages, factories, and even in families. When the deadly madness was over, it was estimated that the campaign against the "enemies of the people" resulted in between eight hundred thousand and five million deaths.

But it was not enough to physically eliminate the bourgeois for the revolution to triumph. Every potential threat to Marxist power and ideology had to be eliminated. Any trace of Western liberal thinking had to be erased from collective memory. One of the main targets of this ideological crusade is the intellectuals. Many espoused Western values and were trained to think independently. The Communist regime, however, couldn't simply eliminate them: it needed their contribution and expertise. So Mao decided on a vast re-education campaign. Tens of thousands of writers, artists, teachers, journalists, and engineers were enrolled in revolutionary colleges where they would spend six to eight months receiving their Marxist education. Since many intellectuals came from wealthy families, party executives taught them to be aware of their class status and to reject it. They took courses on the revolution and studied the texts of Marx, Engels, Lenin, and Stalin as well as the Maoist doctrine. Finally, they were required to participate in self-criticism sessions and write autobiographies in which they analyzed their faults and those of their families. Only when the party deemed their repentance and their rectification sincere were they authorized to hold positions in the new revolutionary China.

The widening gap between the discourse on democracy and the reality of the dictatorship was becoming apparent. The freedoms Mao promised the Chinese to differentiate himself from Chiang Kai-shek's authoritarianism were gradually reduced to nothing or subordinated to the party's group-think. In 1954, Mao abandoned the common program and replaced it with a constitution based on the Soviet model. Like the Soviet constitution, the new Chinese constitution proclaimed the primacy of individual rights. In reality, it served as a smokescreen for the party's repression and dictatorship. Despite Mao's commitment to universal suffrage, the members of the new National People's Congress, which replaced the former parliament, were chosen from a list of candidates drawn up by the Communist Party. As planned, Mao's new democracy was subjected to the sole will of the Communist Party.

In 1956, the young republic was only seven years old; China, in this short period, was undergoing a radical transformation. Agriculture was being collectivized, the country was going ahead with unprecedented industrialization, the structure of the government was modified fundamentally, not to mention the millions of deaths caused by these disruptions. Mao, living in apartments formerly reserved for members of the court, behaved increasingly like an autocrat. His portrait appeared on banknotes and postage stamps, and students sang hymns in praise of the Great Helmsman. In the manner of an emperor, Mao gradually became a paternal figure for a people emerging from a half-century of civil war. He was the bearer of what historian Jonathan Fenby calls, with elegant irony, the "Marxist-Maoist Mandate of Heaven."[8]

The institutions of democratic socialism were rapidly reduced to being institutions in name only. Parliament sat only rarely and merely served to ratify the decisions of the Communist leadership on whom Mao was already imposing his iron will. The Communist leader, satisfied with the results of the first five-year plan, predicted that the socialist revolution now would be completed in three years. Yet the failures of the planned economy soon began to be felt. The peasants, forced to send part of their crop to the cities and to the USSR as a means of payment for agricultural machinery, did not have enough to eat. The new state-owned enterprises were not able to fill the production orders necessitated by industrial catching-up. Rural revolts and workers' strikes increased. The people had no political representation allowing them to make their grievances known. There was tension also in the politburo, and certain members, such as Zhou Enlai, believed the pace of the reforms should be slowed.

This first questioning of the Chinese Revolution came at the moment when Stalin's death thrust the great Communist family into an existential crisis. Stalin's successor, Khrushchev, triggered the revision of Stalinist infallibility with his famous February 1956 speech in which he denounced

Stalin's crimes and cult of personality. A few months later, inspired by Khrushchev's open criticism, the Poles and Hungarians rebelled against the straitjacket imposed by Moscow. Mao supported the Soviets' brutal repression of the Poles and Hungarians. But he also learned an important lesson from the crisis: he believed he had to breathe new life into his revolution by letting intellectuals express themselves. What would follow would be a democratic opening both unpredicted and short-lived, known as the Hundred Flowers Campaign.

On May 2, 1956, Mao gave a speech behind closed doors to eighteen hundred delegates in which he declared that they had to let "a hundred flowers bloom" in terms of culture and "a hundred schools of thought contend" in the sciences. Considering the brutality with which he would later repress the very people he had encouraged to speak their mind, Mao's true intentions would become the object of an academic debate that persists still today: did he naively underestimate discontent among the intellectuals, or did he merely wish to flush out enemies of the party?

Officially, Mao's speech dealt with the correct method for coming to terms with the "contradictions of the people." Outwardly, Mao tried to determine whether he needed to show more openness to avoid the disgraces Stalin had been subjected to since his death and the frustration that led the Poles and Hungarians to rise up against their Communist masters and, by extension, the Soviet leaders. In any case, when Mao invited people to express their grievances, an avalanche of criticism and appeals for democracy followed. At Beijing University, the students erected a Democracy Wall that they covered with posters criticizing the Communist Party. A professor from the province of Hankou denounced the tyranny of the regime and the farce of elections carried out from party-approved lists. He complained that the Chinese knew nothing about the candidates and had become simple voting machines. The criticism didn't only stem from the universities. Mao had inadvertently triggered an intellectual rebellion similar to that of May 4, 1919. Even the official press joined in. The *People's Daily*, one of the party's mouthpieces, announced that from then on it would cover the "socialist and capitalist world," whether it was pleasant or not. Liu Shaoqui, the number-two man in the regime, told journalists to make their publication more interesting for readers and even declared it necessary to protect the rights of the counter-revolutionaries. In several cities in China, students rebelled, beat up party executives, and vandalized their offices. In Shanghai, there were no fewer than eighty-six strikes in 1956. More than ten thousand workers joined a new democratic party. "Let's create another Hungarian Incident!" became a popular working-class slogan, echoing the rebellion in the Eastern bloc countries.

Mao obviously had not anticipated the magnitude or violence of the criticism directed at the Communist regime. The outpouring of dissidence released by the Hundred Flowers Campaign reveals how much, only eight years after the Communist Revolution, many Chinese rejected its premise. There was nothing democratic about Mao's socialism. The people's dictatorship was in fact the tyranny of the party. Mao's reaction was brutal. Only four months after inviting Chinese to criticize the party, he launched a huge anti-rightist campaign to punish those who dared express themselves. Deng Xiaoping was assigned to lead the campaign to, in Mao's terms, "remove the pus from the abscess." More than four hundred thousand intellectuals were persecuted during the summer of 1957. They were branded as right-wingers and subjected to humiliating self-criticism sessions. People accused them of plotting to overthrow the Communist Party and put the "dogs of imperialism" back in power. Thousands were sent to labour camps or prison. Others were forced into the countryside to learn how to work the land. All were put on file, their careers ruined.

To justify his about-turn, Mao literally rewrote history. He had an amended version published of the text in which he had asked the party to allow the Hundred Flowers Campaign to blossom. The new version implied that the expression of intellectual freedom was meant to reinforce socialism, not contest it. The purge of intellectuals was justified by the fact that they abused and made illegitimate use of their freedom of speech. Mao wrote that democracy should not be seen as an end in itself but as a means to resolve differences in the party and among the people. He reminded people that at the time of the revolution the Communist Party had recourse to "Great Liberal Democracy" to fight imperialism and capitalism. But this "Great Democracy" was a means to reach the aims of socialism. There could be no democratic debate challenging the foundations of the revolution or the primacy of the Communist Party. Deng Xiaoping, who thirty years later would crush the Tiananmen Square movement, specified that it was necessary to differentiate between "socialist democracy," which is desirable, and "bourgeois democracy," which is not.[9] Today, this basis of Mao's thoughts on democracy still makes up the foundations of the doctrine applied by Chinese Communist leaders.

Mao was to make a final contribution to the idea of Chinese democracy during the Cultural Revolution of the 1960s by granting the Red Guards what he called "Great Democracy." At the time, China was emerging from the disaster of the Great Leap Forward, when Chinese were taken from their land and relocated in agricultural or industrial communes. Mao's objective was to make China an economic powerhouse able to compete with the West. Party officials even encouraged peasants to melt their utensils, pots and pans, and tools to increase the country's steel production. The Great Leap Forward was a failure: it broke up families, dismantled villages, and impoverished agriculture without giving China the economic and industrial expansion desired by Mao. In the early 1960s, more than thirty million Chinese died of hunger and malnutrition in the aftermath of Mao's Great Leap Forward. Faced with the devastating effects of this policy, some members of the politburo, including President Liu Shaoqi, Party General Secretary Deng Xiaoping, and Zhou Enlai, tried to lead the economy in a more pragmatic direction. The influence of Mao, now more than seventy years old, was waning. Mao was particularly angry at President Liu Shaoqi, who had defied him publicly during the Party Congress regarding the tens of millions of people who died of famine. Liu paid for this affront with his life.

The Cultural Revolution, which began in 1966, was the opportunity for Mao to re-establish his authority over the regime and oust those he considered enemies. Some, such as Deng Xiaoping, had been fellow travellers of Mao since the Long March. Originally, the Cultural Revolution stemmed from the wish of some of Mao's allies and supporters to restore the Great Helmsman's image and fight what they considered the drift toward Westernization in the party and in society. The minister of defence, Lin Biao, set about building up a real cult of Mao. He was responsible for *The Little Red Book* of Mao's thoughts that became the bible of the Red Guards. The other great architect of the Cultural Revolution was Mao's wife, Jiang Qing. A former movie star, she felt that Chinese writers and artists had abandoned the ideals of the revolution and were indirectly using their works to criticize Mao and the party. In the winter of 1966, inspired by Jiang Qing's anti-bourgeois campaign against artists, students at Beijing University took to the streets. The revolt spread rapidly. In August, Mao addressed tens of thousands of Red Guards from atop the entrance to the Forbidden City and gave his official approval to their Cultural Revolution.

Mao concluded that the revolution was losing its momentum and that party officials were losing their impetus. He believed the revolution had to be permanent; it was the only way to make adjustments to a regime that was showing signs of becoming bourgeois. Everything deemed not in accordance with the socialist system and proletarian dictatorship had to be attacked. The Red Guards, who marched in Beijing and the villages brandishing *The Little Red Book,* were encouraged to give free rein to their revolutionary rage and challenge the Four Olds: old ideas, old culture, old customs, and old habits.[10] Schools and universities were closed to allow students to participate in the revolutionary action. They ransacked temples and buildings, destroyed works of art, and attacked people who represented authority in all its forms. Parents, professors, party officials, and superiors were paraded wearing a dunce cap before being subjected to painful and humiliating self-criticism sessions on public platforms. Many died; others were driven to suicide. Mao also decided the purge should apply to the high echelons of the party and government. Dozens of his colleagues and friends and relatives were denounced and dismissed. The cruellest fate was reserved for Liu Shaoqi. The president was dragged outside his home and forced to recite passages from Mao's *Little Red Book*. Liu and his wife were reviled for hours and beaten only a few metres away from Mao's apartments. Mao probably heard them being tortured. Shortly afterward, an editorial in the *People's Daily* accused Liu of being the greatest of capitalists. He was arrested and died of pneumonia in prison in 1969. Mao had him treated by doctors in prison so that he would be alive when he had him expelled from the party.

In order to give legitimacy to this hysterical, arbitrary purge, in which people were accused and put to death without any form of trial, Mao called the Cultural Revolution a "great democracy." This democracy included four great freedoms that gave free rein to the worst violence of the Red Guards: the right to speak out freely, to air views fully, to hold great debates, and to write big-character posters. Mao believed the Cultural Revolution exceeded in importance the 1871 Paris Commune, one of Marxist literature's emblematic proletarian revolts. The Red Guards' maniacal rage, however, was fuelled as much by living conditions under communism as by the ideological failings of party officials. Young people were poor, had few employment perspectives, lived in shoddy apartments with their parents, and were under the domination of corrupt local officials. Their revolt was also that of a frustrated generation. Once his purge was completed, however, Mao no longer needed the Red Guards. He sent them back to school and university, where they had to cast aside the freedom of expression the Great Helmsman had granted them during their revolt. Army officials took top jobs in ministries and institutions. All of Mao's potential rivals were ousted or eliminated. Deng Xiaoping, who would later be called to replace Mao, was deprived of his functions and expelled with his family to the countryside. The final decade of Mao's reign would be characterized by political stagnation and great cultural darkness.

The Cultural Revolution remains in many respects Mao's political legacy. It expresses the last wishes of a man who could not imagine sharing power or integrating dialogue and dissidence into China's political system. By decreeing the revolution should be permanent, Mao made dissension an act of treason. This still has an effect today. If a Chinese blogger calls for democracy or the respect of rights, he or she risks being sentenced to prison for anti-revolutionary acts and attempting to usurp power. During all his years, however, Mao constantly spoke of democracy. He used it as a bait to increase support, as a facade to mask his growing hold on power, and as legitimization for the most terrible violence. The *Party's democracy*, which took the illusory form of *liberal democracy* with the taking of power, became the *new democracy* with the elimination of the bourgeoisie before being transformed into the supreme parody of the *Great Democracy* during the Cultural Revolution. As time went by, the idea of democracy was used by Mao and the Communist Party to justify its opposite. The very term was rendered meaningless. Democracy, in Communist China, meant blind obedience to the party and to Mao's thought. Any dissidence was considered anti-democratic, as it challenged the wisdom of the party through which the will of the people was expressed. That Communist leaders were the only ones empowered to translate the will of the people is not the least of the democratic paradoxes inherited from the Mao era.

Yet this does not mean the Chinese gave up the will to express themselves. Each time Mao loosened the vise of repression ever so slightly, as during the Hundred Flowers Campaign, hundreds of thousands of Chinese came forward to be heard. Intellectuals demanded democracy, workers demanded rights, while in the countryside people demanded something much more basic: justice from the arbitrariness of party officials. The fact they were ready to risk prison and sometimes their lives to express themselves reveals how little recourse the Chinese had in a regime accountable only to itself. As we will see later, the Communist Party's lack of accountability remains today one of the Chinese government's main challenges as it tries to deal with tensions inherent to an emerging capitalist economy that has little room for expression or forums in which grievances can be addressed.

The Cultural Revolution had two unexpected effects on the debate on democracy in China. By temporarily granting the Red Guards freedom of thought and freedom to rebel, Mao inadvertently spawned a desire for democracy that would come back to haunt the party ten years later. By attacking the privileges and corruption of party officials, the Red Guards became aware of the gulf between Communist discourse and reality. Moreover, and this would have significant consequences for the Tiananmen Square tragedy, senior officials in the Communist Party, starting with Deng Xiaoping, were traumatized by the anarchic violence of the Red Guards. In their minds, the idea of democracy would forever be associated with the hoards of youths who swooped down on them and on all symbols of authority in 1966. When students besieged Tiananmen Square in the spring of 1989, Communist leaders had in mind the mob of Red Guards who, on the same square in the summer of 1966, were about to take the country by storm and attack every symbol of authority.

4
Wei Jingsheng's Awakening

Lanzhou, 1967

In the train carrying him far from Beijing and his illusions, Wei Jingsheng, a seventeen-year-old Red Guard, looked out the window at a steady stream of poverty. A few days earlier he had left with some friends who, like him, wanted to discover rural China, the real China, and see if it truly corresponded with the mythical country Mao had painted for them during the Cultural Revolution. For Wei Jingsheng was beginning to have doubts about Mao and socialism. What he saw confirmed his suspicions and appalled him. When the train stopped in a small station in western China, a hoard of beggars rushed to the carriages and held out their hands to passengers. Wei Jingsheng leaned out the window and noticed a girl of about fifteen, covered in soot, begging him for food. He rummaged in his bag and removed a few cakes that he held out to the famished people below. They threw themselves on the food like animals, as if their miserable lives had wiped out any trace of humanity in them. When Wei Jingsheng looked more closely, he noticed that the girl had no clothes; she was completely naked beneath the layer of soot covering her.

More than thirty years later, in the office of the foundation he runs in Washington, D.C., Wei Jingsheng tells me how this scene was a true epiphany for him. It was at that moment he decided not to keep silent, even if it earned him years in prison. He is China's most famous dissident; some people call him the Chinese Nelson Mandela. Imprisoned first in 1979 for his role in the Democracy Wall movement, he was released in 1997 for medical reasons and expelled to the United States. The man is as sturdy as an oak; he seems to carry no trace of the heart problems, ill treatment, and malnutrition that undermined his health in prison. His office, located upstairs in a Victorian house a few streets from American Congress, looks like Ali Baba's cave. I have to make my way among the pile of documents and reports detailing rights violations in China lying about the office. Wei Jingsheng, seated on a worn sofa, smokes one cigarette after another and drinks plenty of tea, like a man who has endured hardship. He knows how to laugh at life and at himself and is a master at irony. After all these years, despite ordeals and reversals that would have discouraged many, his core convictions remain intact, rock solid. An eternal optimist, Wei Jingsheng continues to believe he will soon return home to a democratic China.

At first sight, Wei Jingsheng didn't seem destined to become a dissident, a pariah, an enemy of the Chinese government. Quite the opposite. Born in 1950 in Beijing, only a few months after the founding of Communist China, Wei Jingsheng grew up in a revolutionary family, lulled by his father's Marxist certainties and his mother's socialist humanism. Both were party officials, he in the civil aviation administration, she in the Ministry of Textiles. His father, Wei Zilin, had been bruised by the repression that followed the Hundred Flowers Campaign in 1957, but his career had recovered. The family lived in a residential neighbourhood reserved for party members. The path of Wei Jingsheng and his three brothers and sisters already had been mapped out. They attended the best schools and were promised to be Communist Party members. The family library contained the complete works of Marx, Lenin, Stalin, and, of course, Mao. The young Wei was required to read a page a day before he was allowed to sit down to dinner.[1] When the Cultural Revolution broke out in 1966, he was sixteen and had just finished his secondary studies at the prestigious high school associated with Beijing University. He did not know it, but his whole world was about to be shaken to its core.

Wei Jingsheng spent the spring of 1966 wandering the streets of Beijing, wearing an armband and carrying a *Red Book*, ready to flush out enemies of the people who, according to Mao, threatened the Communist Revolution. Like the other Red Guards, he was drunk on the words of the Great Helmsman. Caught in the frenzy of the times, he had little time for reflection. "I was," said Wei Jingsheng, "a true Maoist fanatic." Later, the Red Guards were sent to the countryside to, in Wei's terms, stir up trouble in schools, ministries, and factories. With time, however, Wei Jingsheng began to have doubts. He wondered how so many party officials could be enemies of the people unless the system itself was corrupt. How could these peasants, who told him they had been starving during the Great Leap Forward, and who today hated the party, all be wrong? Why would a journalist from Beijing, persecuted, disowned by her family, and banished to the countryside, lie when she told him she was innocent?

When the initial wave of the Cultural Revolution began to subside, in early 1967, the Red Guards were left to themselves. A good many of them were sent to the countryside and remained there for years, unable to return home, condemned to a pittance of a job. Many felt they had been manipulated by Mao. Indoctrinated by the propaganda of the Cultural Revolution, they demanded democracy from party officials, but paradoxically, as Wei Jingsheng said, "we scorned democracy, blindly followed the instructions of a dictator." For Wei Jingsheng, it was a time of profound questioning. His journey by train through the Chinese countryside had convinced him there was a huge discrepancy between Communist discourse and reality. He did not yet know if Marxism was to blame, or if party leaders had distorted it. Back in Beijing, with no opportunity to pursue graduate studies, he delved into the works of Marx, Lenin, and Mao to try to find answers to his questions.

Wei Jingsheng reached two conclusions: the Chinese people's real lifestyle was clearly below that of the official propaganda and they had no recourse, no way to make their voices heard by the party. The Communist Revolution, the proletarian dictatorship, and socialist democracy had not kept their promises. "From then on," he said in his autobiography written in prison, and published clandestinely abroad, "when people spoke of the 'superiority of socialism,' in newspapers, I said to myself, 'Bullshit!'"[2] Wei had no access to the classics of Western philosophy that would have provided a political model to compete with the Marxism he had absorbed since his youth and in which he was losing faith. There were copies of Kant's and Rousseau's writings and more recent studies on democracy, but they were under lock and key in party libraries. Thanks to his father's card, Wei Jingsheng managed to borrow some volumes and journals on international politics reserved for the party elite. Rereading Marx and some critical volumes of Marxism written by intellectual dissidents from Eastern Europe, Wei began to form opinions about the inadequacies of socialism and the Chinese people's lack of rights. Contrary to Chinese reformers from the early part of the century, however, Wei had no political agenda; his sense of revolt was more instinctive and less a thoughtful denunciation of injustice. Indeed, there was no continuity between the first Chinese democrats and the young activists who came out of the Cultural Revolution. The writings of Chinese reformers from the beginning of the century, such as Liang Qichao, who thought at length about democracy and tried to imagine its implementation in the Chinese context, were not available. The intellectual capital of democratic reform, which included the notions of individual freedom, fundamental rights, rule of law, and responsible government, apparently had to be rebuilt with each generation. The severing of the genetic link that would unite the people who, over the century, advocated China's democratization has serious consequences still today.

In 1967, Wei briefly joined a group of former demobilized Red Guards who contested the policies of the Cultural Revolution, but they were rapidly dispersed by Mao's wife, Jiang Qing, who received the order to crush the so-called "rebellious children" of the revolution she herself had helped bring into the world. Wei was detained for four months for his participation in the group. When he was released, thanks to family connections, Wei joined the army and was posted in the country's northwest, where he was put in charge of protecting public granaries from attacks by the famished population. In 1973, he returned to Beijing, where he was assigned work as an electrician at the municipal zoo. During all that time, Wei continued his political reflection and constantly promoted democracy among his fellow workers. When the registration period reopened at universities, Wei tried his luck, but his application was rejected. The field he chose likely had something to do with the refusal. He was in love with a Tibetan and wanted to study the history of the Tibetan people, who rose up periodically against the Chinese government. For Wei, as for many Chinese, the decade that separated the Cultural Revolution from Mao's death was a period of stagnation and intellectual emptiness. People were waiting for Mao to die to see if things would change.

Yet it was Zhou Enlai's death in the winter of 1976, six months before Mao's, that triggered a reaction among Beijing's student population. On April 5, 1976, a holiday when the Chinese care for graves, thousands of young people assembled in Tiananmen Square, at the foot of the Monument to the People's Heroes, to pay homage to Zhou Enlai. It was an indirect way of criticizing Mao, since Zhou was considered to be more open and conciliatory than the Great Helmsman. The police intervened and imprisoned the group leaders, including Wang Juntao, the future éminence grise of the Tiananmen Square protestors. Wei Jingsheng did not take part in the demonstrations. He felt that Zhou Enlai was hardly any better than Mao and that it was the whole Marxist system that needed to be changed. The April 5 Incident, as it is now known, served as a prelude to a radical realignment of the country's political forces triggered by Mao's death the following fall. The Great Helmsman's death led to the arrest of the Gang of Four, including Mao's wife, Jiang Qing; they were tried and held responsible for the madness of the Cultural Revolution.

Mao's death also allowed Deng Xiaoping to increase his power and influence. In 1977, he was reinstated as vice-chairman of the Central Committee. Deng's allies now had the upper hand. That signalled a significant change in direction of Chinese leadership. Mao's class struggle gave way to Deng's pragmatism. Deng, championing the need for greater economic flexibility, declared it mattered little whether a cat was "black or white," provided that it knew how to "catch mice." Deng founded his political and economic program on "four modernizations:" agriculture, industry, science, and technology. There was new inspiration, new dynamism in the government. The change in direction Deng wanted China to take was fundamental. He placed Hu Yaobang, one of his most loyal allies, in charge of building a new political infrastructure to support his new pragmatism. Essentially, Deng understood that economic projections could not continue to stem from Communist ideology. This was the kind of reasoning that led to the error of the Great Leap Forward and accounted for China's industrial backwardness. When in the fall of 1978 the Central Committee decreed that hundreds of thousands of victims of the Cultural Revolution and the Anti-Rightist Campaign of the late 1950s had been unjustly persecuted and were reinstated and that the April 5, 1976, movement was retrospectively considered legitimate, it essentially repudiated Mao's governing principles. Party officials who were persecuted during the Cultural Revolution returned to Beijing, where many of them were reinstated in the government. With Deng, they wanted to reform the Communist Party so as to prevent the appearance of a cult of personality, like the one that under Mao led to aberrations such as the Cultural Revolution. As any reform or repression in China usually took the form of a campaign or a movement, the one aiming to free the country from Mao's legacy was named the Thought Emancipation Movement.

With Deng's return, the Chinese sensed a new tolerance for political reflection. In the days following the announcement of the rehabilitation of those imprisoned for their role in the April 5 incident, posters began to appear on a large grey brick wall on Chang'an Avenue, to the west of Tiananmen Square. Taking advantage of the new climate of openness, people met at the foot of the wall to discuss reform and put up posters demanding more transparency in the party. Often these were indirect criticisms of Mao. Posters of this sort have a long tradition in China. Young intellectuals at the beginning of the century used them to contest the Qing Dynasty, and so did the members of the Modernization Movement of May 4, 1919. In December 1978, many Chinese used the posters to show support for Deng Xiaoping. He, incidentally, unequivocally approved the Democracy Wall. "The people want to speak," he said in a rare interview he gave American journalist Robert Novak, "let them. We do not have the right to deny or criticise the blossoming of democracy and the posters."[3] The only freedom of expression and democracy Deng Xiaoping was prepared to tolerate, however, was that which did not question the Communist Party's legitimacy and its monopoly of power. He was merciless with those who, like Wei

Jingsheng, would dare venture into that restricted area. Ultimately, the criticisms posted on the Democracy Wall, inasmuch as they respected prescribed limits, were a good thing for Deng Xiaoping. As Mao had done before him, he invoked the people's dissatisfaction to overcome the resistance of reactionary elements in the party. During a preparatory meeting for the Third Plenum of the Central Committee in the fall of 1978, Deng bluntly warned the party that if it did not find a means to respond to the dissatisfaction of the people, who were beginning to express themselves it in the street, its survival was at stake.

Some evenings, when his shift at the Beijing Zoo was over, Wei Jingsheng would go to the Democracy Wall. While he was delighted to see that the Chinese dared express themselves, he was disappointed by how timid their words were and by their naiveté. He was particularly outraged by a poster written by students demanding protesters follow Deng's slogan and return to schools or factories. In Wei's eyes, this was proof that by tolerating the Democracy Wall, Deng was only seeking to consolidate his power at the expense of the conservatives. Deng Xiaoping's modernization program, he believed, was just a new way of justifying the Communist Party's dictatorship. It didn't get to the bottom of things. So, on the evening of December 4, 1978, Wei took a paintbrush and ink and in big characters wrote what would become the political manifesto of his generation. It took him all night to complete his poster that he hung the following morning on the Democracy Wall. The text was entitled "The Fifth Modernization." In it, Wei stated that the four modernizations proposed by Deng Xiaoping had no meaning unless they were backed up by a fifth modernization: democracy.

Wei then went to have breakfast in a local restaurant. When he returned a few hours later, a large group had gathered around his poster. People were stunned by the boldness of this electrician, a man of no consequence who so casually dared to contest publicly the emerging consensus around Deng's modernizations. Until then, Chinese who had dared to criticize had done so indirectly, through literary metaphors or by comparing Mao to the first emperors, never naming him. Wei Jingsheng's revolt marked a turning point both in the tone and substance of the criticism. The Chinese Communist Party, he wrote with iconoclastic bluntness, betrayed the people's confidence; its socialist democracy was nothing more than a dictatorship from which the Chinese had to free themselves. Democracy, Wei continued, is an innate right. And what is democracy? It is the right of the people to "choose representatives to manage affairs on the people's behalf and in accordance with the will and interests of the people. This alone can be called democracy. Furthermore, the people must have the power to replace these representatives at any time in order to keep them from abusing their powers to oppress the people." Wei Jingsheng's text challenged the very foundations of the Communist regime, its claim to speak in the name of the people, as well as its monopoly on power.

With disarming simplicity, Wei also gave a whole new dimension to the arguments of those who, for close to a century, had been demanding China's democratization. For Wei, democracy was a natural, innate right of human beings. "The people," Wei wrote, "should have democracy. When they call for democracy they are demanding nothing more than that which is inherently theirs. Whoever refuses to return democracy to them is a shameless thief more despicable than any capitalist who robs the workers of the wealth earned with their own sweat and blood."[4] Until then, Chinese reformers, influenced by the Confucian tradition of social harmony, had always tempered the exercise of democratic right with the necessity of exercising it so as to preserve social harmony. The desires of the individual had to subordinate to the interests of the group. It was this fear of social chaos, this unpredictable side of democracy in particular, that had so troubled Sun Yat-sen, leading him to conclude the Chinese were not ready for democracy. Wei Jingsheng turned this idea on its head. Democracy, he asserted, is not a right to be granted depending on circumstances but an inalienable right, a right that takes precedence over everything else. And it is wrong, he continued, to think that exercising it degenerates necessarily into popular chaos. "Will the country sink into chaos and anarchy if the people achieve democracy?" asked Wei. "On the contrary," he said. "Those who worry that democracy will lead to anarchy and chaos are just like those who, following the overthrow of the Qing dynasty, worried that without an emperor, the country would fall into chaos."[5] Wei ended his charge by coming back to the title of his poster. Without a fifth modernization, embodied by democracy, the four modernizations proposed by Deng Xiaoping were condemned to fail. "Without democracy," concluded Wei, "society will become stagnant and economic growth will face insurmountable obstacles."[6] The affront to Deng Xiaoping and his renewal project could not have been any clearer. Later, when someone suggested to Wei that he meet Deng to discuss their differences, Wei added insult to injury. "He has no legal status by which to talk to me," retorted Wei. "He was not elected by the people."

Wei was very conscious of the impact of his actions and words. He knew he was exposing himself to severe reprisals. Despite this, he wrote his phone number on the bottom of his poster. "Young people phoned me because they wanted to organize an action group," Wei says. "I told them to think about it for three days because it was risky. 'Are you ready to die for it?' I asked them. 'For a country to change, it takes people ready to sacrifice themselves. If you are ready to do that, follow me.' Three days later, three of the thirteen young people had decided to remain." Repression, when it came, would be merciless, but that would be later. In December 1978, all of China seemed carried by a wind of reform. While the Chinese painted their posters and put them up on the Democracy Wall, Deng Xiaoping urged the Communist Party to accept his modernization program. If there were doubts about the direction in which Deng intended to steer the country, they were quickly dispelled by the announcement, on December 19, three days before the end of the plenum of the party, that the government would buy three Boeing 747s from the United States. The same day, the Coca-Cola Company announced it had just obtained permission from the Chinese government to sell its iconic beverage in China.

These announcements set the stage for Deng's historic visit to the United States the following month. On January 1, 1979, the United States and China restored diplomatic relations. On January 28, Deng Xiaoping flew to Washington, where he began a triumphant tour of the United States. Americans welcomed this new Chinese leader with open arms. He was so different from Mao in height and temperament, and seemed determined to bring China in step with the international community. Deng was hosted by Jimmy Carter at the White House, visited a Ford Company factory and the New York Stock Exchange, played with the controls of a NASA space shuttle flight simulator, and, sporting a cowboy hat, posed in a rodeo. These images were widely distributed in China, where they had a resounding effect. Returning to Beijing, inspired by his economic modernization program and his ideological pragmatism, Deng, behind the closed doors of the Central Committee, mused out loud about the destiny of socialist democracy. Proletarian democracy, he said, referring to Marxist vocabulary, must surpass capitalist democracy. In Deng's mind, however, democracy had to be exercised within the Communist Party. He did not tolerate any questioning of the party's monopoly of power nor any overly severe criticism of its regime and its leadership. Shortly afterward, the fiasco of the attempted invasion of Vietnam by the Chinese army in the winter of 1979 heralded the end of the opening that allowed for the appearance of the Democracy Wall. When the Chinese began painting posters criticizing China's aggression against Vietnam, Deng decided that he'd had enough.[7] Security forces prepared to put an end to the Democracy Wall.

In less than two months, however, the movement had taken on dimensions that largely went beyond putting up slogans on a grey brick wall in Beijing. Democracy Walls appeared in many cities in China. Dozens of journals and magazines appeared whose circulation allowed them to reach even more Chinese. They had evocative titles such as *Beijing Spring*, *Human Rights in China*, and *Democracy and Law*. In the wake of the success of his *dazibao*, his big character poster, Wei Jingsheng, with friends, founded his own journal, *Exploration* (*Tansuo* in Chinese). The magazine's mission was to propagate "freedom of speech, publication, and association as provided by the Constitution." Wei gave up his electrician job at the zoo; he spent most of his time producing his journal, which he printed in his apartment on a duplicating machine. It was an exhilarating adventure. He spent long days and nights mapping out the political future with his friends and colleagues. Wei also spent a lot of time finding enough paper to print his magazine. Paper was controlled, and Wei often had to call on sympathetic contacts in government printing offices who gave him a supply. Over time, Wei developed and explored in greater depth the ideas he had set out in his manifesto "The Fifth Modernization." We have only to look at the hovels in which people live, he wrote in one of his essays, as well as the prostitution, poverty, and begging, to conclude that in thirty years the Communist Party has not managed to settle China's economic and social problems. The collectivism of the world's socialist countries, he continued, is a failure because it leaves no room for individualism.

The frustration of the Chinese was not only expressed in posters and magazines; it also began to spill into the streets. It seemed that all over the country the Chinese were taking advantage of the current atmosphere of openness to demonstrate. Many were youths who had been sent to the country in the wake of the Cultural Revolution. At the beginning of January 1979, a few thousand of them converged on Beijing, brandishing banners proclaiming: "We don't want hunger" and "We want human rights and democracy."[8] In Shanghai, a group of demonstrators besieged the offices of the Communist Party. In Hangzhou, people demanded the right to live like "human beings." Wei Jingsheng was aware the Communist leaders would not tolerate such outbursts for long. His contacts in the security forces forewarned him that they had received instructions to prepare plans to put an end to the Democracy Wall and arrest its leaders. "I have known the Communists since I was very young," Wei Jingsheng tells me between two cigarettes. "First, they resort to democracy to overcome resistance in the party, then they use the army to place themselves in a more authoritarian position and establish their power. The message they send is that they will not hesitate to eliminate opposition inside and outside the party. From the moment Deng overcame the resistance inside the party, I knew from sources in the security system that he intended to eliminate the Democracy Wall."

There were other indications of imminent repression. Municipal authorities in Beijing declared restrictions on public meetings and limited demonstrations to an area around the Democracy Wall. The *People's Daily* warned those who criticized Communist Party officials that their "actions would be vigorously repressed." According to the newspaper, they distorted the meaning of democracy. "The kind of democracy we need is socialist democracy.... We don't want bourgeois democracy, which enables a handful of people to oppress the majority of people."[9]

Sporadic arrests took place, mostly of people who wrote in underground magazines. On March 16, in a speech to the party behind closed doors, Deng gave orders to knock down the Democracy Wall and severely punish its activists; he called them counter-revolutionaries working for Taiwan and supporters of the Gang of Four. Deng probably still remembered the chaos of the Cultural Revolution; he feared his political plans would be undermined by criticism and demonstrations. He said that if they did not put an end to all that abstract talk around democracy, it would perhaps lead to "ultra-democracy and anarchism, to the disruption of political stability and unity and to the total failure of our modernization campaign."

Rumours of imminent arrests spread in the capital. Authorities published an edict forbidding slogans, posters, books, magazines, photographs, and any other material that challenged socialism, the proletarian dictatorship, the leaders of the Communist Party, Marxism-Leninism, or the thoughts of Mao Zedong. The Democracy Wall and the new magazines that appeared in its wake were outlawed. An informal liaison committee of various journals met to think about how to react to what was, for all practical purposes, the death sentence of their movement. From the outset, Wei Jingsheng suggested publicly exposing and denouncing the campaign of repression. Some people, such as Liu Qing, of the *April 5 Forum*, claimed it would only exacerbate the regime's anger. Thirty years later, exiled in the United States, Wei Jingsheng tells me of his motivations and strategy at the time: "The minister of public security intended to arrest at least thirty-six people. It would be the end of the Democracy Wall. I told the group it was impossible for us to avoid it; there was only one way to save the Democracy Wall. Rather than seeking to appease Deng Xiaoping, we had to aggravate him more and defy him. That would lead to more arrests, but the world would learn what was really happening in China."

The difference between Wei and the other reformists was more than about strategy. Many of them still saw themselves in the traditional role of the Chinese intellectual that involved advising the emperor and leading him to correct his errors. They still believed in socialism, in the democracy of the party. This was shattered under Mao, but they believed that with the arrival of Deng and his modernization program it would be possible to promote greater democracy and greater transparency within the government. The difference with Wei Jingsheng is that he had lost faith in socialism. In his eyes, the system could not be reformed. While others spoke of invoking the constitution to convince authorities of the validity of the Democracy Wall movement, Wei opted for confrontation. He told them he would act alone if necessary. It was the strategy of a dissident, some would say of a martyr.

On March 25, two days after a ban was announced on criticizing the party, Wei Jingsheng published a scathing editorial in his magazine, *Exploration*. Titled "Do We Want Democracy or a New Autocracy?" Wei warned the Chinese that Deng was on his way to becoming a dictator, like Mao before him. "Does Deng want democracy?" Wei asked rhetorically. "No, he does not. He says that the spontaneous struggle for democratic rights is just an excuse to make trouble, that it destroys the normal order and must be suppressed." Wei knew that with such a crime of lèse-majesté, he had just crossed an unacceptable threshold. That was in fact his intention. But he also had another objective. "I wanted to warn party members that Deng was building up a dictatorship," he tells me. "That would not end well for them. They actually were well aware of that, having experienced the same thing under Mao." Wei knew he was exposing himself to serious reprisals and even, he believed, to the death penalty. Wei also was anxious to protect the people who worked at the magazine with him. He told them to testify against him if they were called upon to do so. He wanted to bear the responsibility for his actions alone.

Four days later, on March 29, a group of twenty police officers appeared at Wei's home in the middle of the night and arrested him. He was held for the next six months in a section reserved for people sentenced to death in Beijing's gloomy Banbuqiao prison. "What allowed me to survive was that I didn't expect to live," he told me. "According to Communist custom, people who criticized the party so openly had no chance of survival. Before the Democracy Wall, even moderates who criticized the party were killed." On October 16, 1979, Wei appeared before a Beijing court. He was accused of divulging military secrets to a foreigner about the war against Vietnam and creating counter-revolutionary propaganda with the intent of overthrowing the socialist system. The public prosecutor, dressed in military uniform and white gloves, brandished a copy of *Exploration* as part of the incriminating evidence. "Rule by socialist law," the public prosecutor declared, enumerating the accusations against Wei, "is the embodiment of the will of the proletariat.... If we allow freedom for such a tiny minority to spread unchecked as it pleases, the larger number of the population run the risk of losing their own freedoms." The prosecutor told him, "Our constitution stipulates that you have freedom of belief, and that means you may believe or disbelieve Marxism-Leninism-Mao Zedong Thought, but it also states you are definitely forbidden to oppose it — for opposition is a violation of the constitution."[10] Neither his family nor his lawyer were allowed to attend the trial, which was held behind closed doors. Wei prepared his own defence, which he considered to be his testament. "I was convinced," he told me, "that this was my last chance to express myself."

The verdict left little doubt. Wei appeared in court with his head shaved and dressed in a prisoner's uniform, telltale signs of his imminent guilt. Standing in the dock, Wei refuted the government's accusations one by one. His actions, he declared, were in accordance with Article 45 of the Chinese Constitution, which specifically guaranteed citizens freedom of speech, of publication, and freedom to assemble, demonstrate, hold debates, and produce big character posters. Wei maintained that these freedoms had been eroded, especially at the time of the Cultural Revolution, and that only by restoring these rights and democracy could China be successful in its modernization. The conservative autocrats in the party, he said, were the "true counter-revolutionaries" because they opposed the revolution necessary for democracy. As for the accusation that he wanted to overthrow the government, Wei deemed it absurd. He said he never was part of any conspiracy whatsoever nor did he take part in the activities of an organization dedicated to violence. "Overthrowing the government is not the same as establishing a democratic government," he said. "Perhaps the members of the Procuratorate do not agree with my theory," he concluded, "but their disagreement with my theories does not brand me as someone wanting to overthrow the socialist system."[11]

As expected, his defence had little influence on the court. Wei was sentenced to fifteen years in prison, after which he was stripped of his political rights for three years. Through his reactionary articles, his anti-revolutionary propaganda, and his agitation, said the judge, Wei Jingsheng violated the constitution and endangered public interest. The fact he did not admit to his crimes was an aggravating circumstance that likely explained the heavy sentence he was given. Rumour was that Deng Xiaoping himself had dictated Wei's sentence and his conditions of imprisonment. While his trial took place in secret, the announcement of his sentencing was widely broadcast, and even on loudspeakers in factories. Wei Jingsheng's sentencing served as a warning. As the Chinese saying goes: "Kill the monkey to scare the tiger."

Wei's trial had repercussions beyond China. Soviet dissident Andrei Sakharov sent a telegram to Chinese premier Hua Guofeng, urging him to revise Wei Jingsheng's sentence. In Beijing, Wei's allies tried to broadcast his arguments before the court as widely as possible. Liu Qing managed to obtain a recording of Wei's plea that he published in the *April 5 Forum*. He paid dearly for it: he was arrested and put in prison. Wei was taken to Banbuqiao Detention Centre. He was not allowed visitors and could not read or write or even correspond with his friends and family. By mutual agreement, Wei and his Tibetan fiancée put an end to their union. Wei's fellow prisoners were regularly sent by the guards to beat him. No one was authorized to speak to him. One more form of isolation. In 1981, he was transferred to Beijing Municipal No. 1 Prison. For two years, he was not allowed to leave his cell. After five years of imprisonment, Wei had almost lost the use of his vocal chords. He suffered from high blood pressure, arthritis, and had lost teeth due to deficiencies in the diet to which he was subjected. A prison doctor concluded that his prison conditions were life-threatening. In 1984, he was finally transferred at his request to a labour camp in Qinghai, in western China. His prison conditions improved but only barely: he was allowed to write, have contact with other political prisoners, including former Red Guards, and raise a few rabbits in the prison yard. In all those years, Wei Jingsheng refused to admit his offences or sign any confession, despite daily pressure from the authorities. "They try to make you give up your dreams, your ideal. If that happens, you lose your dignity and that is the end," he says.

In the spring of 1989, ten years after being sent to jail, Wei Jingsheng followed on television from his cell the student demonstrations in Tiananmen Square. Chinese television, inspired by the student movement, momentarily lifted its own censor and openly broadcast what was happening. One might think Wei would have been thrilled that so many young people, a decade after the Democracy Wall, were taking up the torch of reform and continuing the struggle that he himself began. In Wei's eyes, however, the students were very imperfect heirs of his struggle, even though he was flattered that their first demand to authorities was his release. Twenty years later, his verdict on the students' naivety was full of pity but without indulgence.

WJ: The root of the problem, in 1989, was that the students still hoped the regime would agree to reform. Even ordinary Chinese had understood that the Communist Party had to be overthrown, but the students said, "Let's negotiate with the party."

MC: That's the tradition; everyone wants to advise the emperor.

WJ: If the leaders of the movement weren't even ready to sacrifice themselves, how can you expect society to change? On one hand, Deng Xiaoping intends to kill you; on the other, you keep dreaming, sitting in Tiananmen Square. I was in prison in Qinghai then. But the older guards knew what was going to happen. They said to me: if only you were there to help, that would be good. I asked them why. Because the students still have illusions about the Communist Party, they replied.

MC: Even your guards wanted change?

WJ: Everyone wanted China to change.

MC: It must have been frustrating for you. Here was your chance, your moment, and you weren't there.

WJ: Indeed.

MC: What was going through your mind at that moment?

WJ: We all knew that Deng was going to fire on the people.

MC: Did you feel bad for not being there? Did you think you could have made a difference?

WJ: Of course. Everyone thought that. Not just me. Even the police. During the movement for democracy in 1989, we needed clear thinking and determination. Unfortunately the student leaders were deluding themselves. They hoped that one day they would be ministers or senior civil servants in a reformed government. That's why this movement for democracy failed. When you don't have a specific goal, when you don't know your enemy, you are condemned to fail.

Outraged by the military attack against the demonstrators in Tiananmen Square, Wei Jingsheng wrote a long letter to Deng Xiaoping from his cell, one of many he sent to the Communist leader during his incarceration. The tone of the letter, which surely never left the prison walls, was equally sarcastic and scathing. "So, now that you've successfully carried out a military coup to deal with a group of unarmed and politically inexperienced students and citizens, how do you feel?" he asked Deng Xiaoping. Then he accused him of betraying the democratic ideal of the revolution by becoming a tyrant and a dictator. "In your heart you know what a great mistake you have made...it appears you would rather die than admit that you were wrong."[12]

Shortly after, Wei was transferred to a labour camp, the Nanpu Salt Works, where his prison conditions worsened. He was not allowed to wash for months and was forbidden any contact with other prisoners. Wei carried out a series of hunger strikes, the longest of which lasted close to a hundred days, during which time he fed himself on just one a cube of sugar each day. Outside China, following the events of Tiananmen Square, the pressure to free political prisoners was growing stronger. Suddenly, on September 14, 1993, a few months before the end of his sentence, Wei was released but refused to leave the prison without his correspondence, including the many letters he had written to Deng Xiaoping and other Chinese leaders. His release came only a few days before the International Olympic Committee was to reach a decision on Beijing's candidacy for the 2000 Summer Games. Wei shrugged off warnings from authorities not to give interviews to foreign journalists. As soon as he left prison, he told the *New York Times* that it was "dirty and abnormal" to exchange the freedom of a political prisoner for the Olympic Games.

Wei was violating the conditions of his release with almost suicidal nonchalance. He was forbidden to speak to the media, express his opinions, do business, or participate in any organization whatsoever until the end of his conditional release, scheduled for March 1994. Far from submitting to these restrictions, Wei announced he would continue to fight for China's democratization and for the respect of rights and that he even intended to sue the government for having sentenced him unfairly. He lived with his parents. Despite failing health, he had more and more meetings with other dissidents and stayed up late at night. On November 18, the day before the summit between Bill Clinton and Chinese leader Jiang Zemin, Wei wrote an article in the *New York Times* in which he urged the United States to increase pressure on China to respect citizens' rights. He ignored the warnings of the police, who threatened to arrest him again. Three months later he dined with John Shattuck, assistant secretary of state for human rights in the United States: this was one affront too many for the Chinese government. Shortly after, while returning by car from Tianjin, Wei was intercepted by police and held in secret detention. His family had no news of him for close to two years. Finally, in November 1995, Wei was formally accused of "illegal activities under the cloak of legality." The indictment, almost two thousand pages long, criticized him for his writings in prison, his efforts to promote rights and democracy, and for encouraging the United States to put pressure on China. He was also criticized for drawing up lists of names of "political victims," for buying shares in a financial institution, and for planning an art exhibition. In his defence, Wei declared that nothing had changed since the Cultural Revolution. "Promoting rights and democracy and fighting enemies do not constitute a crime," he declared before the court. After a brief pause for lunch, Wei was sentenced to fourteen years in prison. For a while he was incarcerated under constant surveillance in a glass cell.

With this second sentencing, Wei Jingsheng was more than a Chinese dissident; he had become a symbol for the universal struggle for democracy, just like Nelson Mandela and Vaclav Havel. He was nominated for the Nobel Peace Prize, an initiative the Chinese government denounced, saying that a criminal cannot be eligible for such an honour. Nevertheless, two years after his sentencing, in September 1997, Wei was escorted to Beijing Airport and put on board an airplane headed for Detroit. His release, for medical reasons, occurred two weeks after General Secretary Jiang Zemin's visit to the United States. His imprisonment had become a major irritant in relations between China and the United States. Wei had refused previous offers of exile by the Chinese government, but his many health problems following the difficult conditions of his imprisonment led him to agree to leave China, which he had always considered to be a form of surrender.

The journey of self-discovery he had begun on a train leaving Beijing at age seventeen ultimately led him to a life of exile he neither wished nor chose. Along his journey, thanks to an unwavering commitment to his ideals, Wei put up new signposts for the debate on democracy in China. Democracy for him was not a privilege to be granted to the people when they are deemed mature enough to exercise it, nor was it a justification of socialism that does not allow the right to vote outside the Communist Party. It was an inalienable human right that will tolerate no compromise. With Wei, the idea of democracy in China, after being tossed about on the agitated political seas of the century, somehow found its way home to the port of its origins.

5
Bao Tong's Fall

Beijing, May 28, 1989

Wedged between two police officers in the back seat of a car, Bao Tong tries to find his bearings so he can figure out where he's being taken, but it's impossible. The driver has turned so many times and taken so many detours to avoid protesters blocking the area around Tiananmen Square that Bao no longer knows which way the car is headed. He asks the police officers to tell him where they are taking him, but they remain silent. Understandably, they feel intimidated by Bao Tong. They are not dealing with a common criminal but with one of the senior leaders of the Communist Party. Bao is the assistant of Zhao Ziyang, the general secretary of the party and number two in the regime after Deng Xiaoping. He is also the director of the Office of Political Reform mandated by Deng to put China on the road to greater democratization.

But all that is no longer important. In the struggle between students and the government, Bao and Zhao Ziyang sided with the students, who are demanding an end to corruption and more transparency from the government. They have been occupying Tiananmen Square for more than a month. Bao will pay dearly for it and he knows it. His superior, Zhao Ziyang, was also arrested. Both will be held personally responsible for encouraging the student revolt and betraying the party. Bao's service record, the importance of his position, the fact that he was mandated by Deng to explore the question of political reform; none of that matters anymore. Sitting in the backseat of the police car, Bao Tong nevertheless feels serene. "I lived through the Cultural Revolution," he tells me. "I knew that in China anything can happen."

After leaving downtown and going through the suburbs, they end up after an hour's drive in the countryside. In the distance, Bao sees the mountains surrounding the city. They arrive in front of a metal gate. The car stops and the police officers signal to Bao to get out. Three men are waiting near the entrance. "Am I at Qincheng Prison?" Bao asks. Qincheng is the famous prison reserved for political prisoners. "Yes, you are," replies one of the men, "and I'm the warden." Bao asks them if they want to speak to him. "We don't even know who you are," the prison warden replies. Then he hands Bao Tong a register and asks him to write his name in it. Bao Tong does so and hands the register back to the warden. "This is not your name," he says. "From now on, your name is number 8901." Bao Tong understands. He is the first political prisoner of 1989, and for the Chinese government, from then on he is nothing more than a number.

Following the Tiananmen Square trials, Bao Tong was convicted of revealing state secrets and sentenced to seven years in prison. After his release, he spent a year in another place of detention. Since then, he has been under house arrest in Beijing. He is allowed to go out to do his shopping but is under constant surveillance and his phone is tapped. For a journalist, visiting him is a gamble. When I show up with an interpreter at his building, two police officers seated at a desk at the entrance ask for our cards. They jot down our contact information in a large notebook. They are polite, a bit indifferent, but appearances can be deceiving. A few days earlier, they stopped a British television crew from going in. We are approaching the twentieth anniversary of Tiananmen Square and authorities are on the alert. After a few minutes, one of the police officers tells us to phone Bao Tong, who must escort us personally up to his apartment on the sixth floor.

He arrives, modestly dressed in a blue cotton jacket, the kind many retirees wear. His glasses are a little too large, like in the Communist era. At seventy-six, his gait is fragile. He greets the police officers who deprive him of his freedom on a daily basis with no noticeable bitterness. Then he leads us to the elevator. The man exudes undeniable dignity. His demeanour suggests he was once important.

I have many questions to ask Bao Tong. Because he was one of the main architects of the political reforms of the 1980s, the ones that were supposed to accompany economic liberalization, only Bao can tell me how far he and

Zhao Ziyang were ready to go on the road to democratization. As a privileged witness to discussions inside the Communist Party, he is one of the few people who knew Deng Xiaoping's true intentions before the Tiananmen Square crisis led him to slow down the momentum of his own political reforms. He was also one of the few former government leaders to experience Tiananmen from the inside and who dares talk about it. I want to know if he thinks things could have been different. While it is futile to try to imagine what history could have been had the army not intervened in Tiananmen Square, it is fair to say that the "June 4 Incident," as it is now called in China, shaped the Chinese society of today. And that of all the century's democratization movements in China, the wind of reform the country experienced in the 1980s was perhaps the one most likely to launch it on the paths of economic and political liberalization.

Sitting in his modest apartment a stone's throw away from the places where these events occurred, Bao Tong embodies, by the tragic turn his life took, China's failed opportunity. He is a clear-headed man, little drawn to self-pity or the comfort of nostalgia. In December 2008, he took part in writing and, along with three hundred other Chinese intellectuals, signed Charter 08, a manifesto demanding the respect of rights and the democratization of China. This initiative was inspired by Charter 77, which, at the end of the 1970s, formed a pocket of opposition to the Czechoslovakian Communist regime. Bao Tong knew he was exposing himself to further difficulties by committing this act, although security services could not make his life much more miserable, he tells me. The reason he wants to continue fighting, even at his age, he adds, is to correct the error of joining the Communist Party sixty years ago, and beacause he hopes his actions will help create a more open China for his son, his daughter, and his granddaughter.

n the mid-1980s, when Bao Tong worked as director of the Office of Political Reform, China was embracing everything from the West: its music, fashion, and, to some extent, its ideas. In the streets of cities like Shanghai and Beijing, stands selling newspapers and everyday items appeared. The Chinese were making a first, hesitant step toward a market economy. Young people who could afford it bought jeans; the blue cotton tunic that was the symbol of consensus and Communist anonymity gave way to more freedom of expression in terms of fashion. Many students, encouraged by Deng Xiaoping to study abroad, returned full of ideas about how to modernize China. Deng's slogan, according to which the Chinese from now on should seek truth "in facts" and not in Mao's ideology, opened the doorway to greater freedom of thought. At first glance, it may seem surprising that the impetus for change originated with Deng Xiaoping. The aging Deng was eighty years old, a veteran of the revolution and one of the last remaining survivors of the Long March. His entire life had been defined by the fight to make China a Communist success. But Deng was also a pragmatist and knew, at a gut level, that the socialist economy had not kept its promises. Furthermore, when he encouraged students and party officials to go abroad and see how things worked, he was putting them on the path he himself had taken at the start of the century when, with thousands of other young Chinese, he went to France to participate in a work-study program.[1] He worked in a Renault auto plant and in restaurant kitchens in Paris. Witnessing first-hand the poor labour conditions of French workers is what made him a Communist. When he left for France in the summer of 1919, his father asked him what he intended to do there. "To use the knowledge and truth I will find in the West in order to save China," he replied. Deng was echoing the May Fourth Movement that had demonstrated a few months earlier in Tiananmen Square in favour of China's scientific modernization and democratization.

More than a half-century later, at the beginning of the 1980s, Deng found himself back to square one in a way. He launched his four modernizations in the hope that China would catch up with the West and even encouraged the sale of television sets so the Chinese would become aware that their country needed serious help to work up to the level of development of other countries. The Communist leader understood that to survive, the Communist regime had to allow the Chinese a degree of economic freedom, and to ensure its legitimacy, the party had to reform and be more transparent in its operations and decisions and show more democracy in its proceedings and internal elections.

But reform was a slippery slope. The experience of the Democracy Wall, and in particular the case of Wei Jingsheng, showed to what extent the slightest opening could trigger forces difficult for the government to contain. In addition, after Wei was arrested and the Democracy Wall closed down, Deng came to the conclusion that the economic liberalization necessary for China's growth had to be controlled by a political straitjacket. He stated the four cardinal principles that left no doubt as to the limits of the political reforms he contemplated: pre-eminence of Marxism-Leninism and the thought of Mao, the socialist path, dictatorship of the people, and the most important principle, the Communist Party's monopoly of power. A Shanghai radio station used the following image to speak of Deng's four principles. Democracy is like basketball, the host explained. It is played inside a well-defined space. Then, in order to guard against any of his policies being challenged outside the party, Deng revoked the four freedoms Mao had granted the Red Guards during the Cultural Revolution, which were the pillars of what he had called Great Democracy: the right to speak out freely, air views fully, hold great debates, and write big-character posters. These rights, incidentally, had been invoked in their defence by Wei Jingsheng and the protagonists of the Democracy Wall.

Simultaneously, Deng led a fierce battle to impose his new economic philosophy inside the party. Several members of the politburo loyal to Mao still believed in the virtues of a planned economy and refused to endorse the liberalization advocated by Deng. The main obstacle was Hua Guofeng, whom Mao had designated as his successor before he died. "With you in charge, I am at ease,"[2] Mao had scrawled on a piece of paper when he began to lose strength. Hua was not a brilliant man yet had proved himself to be a loyal and skilled administrator who did not threaten to outshine Mao as his reign came to a close. But he was also an official who could not imagine life outside Mao's dogma.

Deng pulled out all the stops at the beginning of the 1980s by forcing Hua Guofeng's main allies to resign from the party's Central Committee. This opened the way for Deng's protégés to be promoted. Hu Yaobang became general secretary and Zhao Ziyang was appointed premier. Hu was a small man, like Deng, and also a veteran of the Long March. He had great intellectual curiosity, devoured foreign books, and liked to travel through the country to see for himself the conditions in which people lived. Deng entrusted Hu with the mission of reforming the party. Zhao Ziyang represented the next generation of leaders. He was born in Hunan into a merchant family and rapidly rose through the ranks of the Communist administration. As leader of Guangdong Province, Zhao, then only forty years old, was severely taken to task during the Cultural Revolution. The Red Guard paraded him in the streets wearing a dunce cap, then relegated him to manual work as a fitter in a Hunan factory. The fact he had been persecuted during the Cultural Revolution was seen positively by Deng, who had also suffered that ignominy. Later rehabilitated, Zhao had proved himself as a strongman and a reformer of Sichuan Province. He shunned Communist doctrine by allowing farmers to sell the surplus of their crop on the local market. Deng soon noticed the young administrator with the round face and big glasses and summoned him to Beijing to lead the series of economic reforms. Ten years later, their boldness, which had so pleased Deng, led Hu Yaobang and Zhao Ziyang to their ruin. Hu, demoted by Deng, who had become suspicious of his loyalty to Communist ideals, died in disgrace. It was his death, in the spring of 1989, that first drew the students to protest at Tiananmen Square.

At the beginning of the 1980s, however, it was smooth sailing for Hu and Zhao. In party circles, Zhao was already perceived as the one to succeed Deng Xiaoping. In order to liberalize the economy and reform the political machine, Zhao was quick to recruit rising stars who thought like him, bold people who would dare stand up to the reactionary elements in the party and embrace new ideas. Bao Tong fit this profile in all respects, and Zhao quickly gave him significant responsibilities. As the premier's personal secretary, he wrote most of Zhao's speeches. Zhao also appointed him director of the Office of Political Reform of the Central Committee of the Communist Party, an office set up to determine what kind of political reforms should accompany the economy's growing liberalization. Finally, Bao was designated as the chief writer of the proposals to be submitted to the 13th Congress of the Communist Party, where the future of the reforms of Zhao Ziyang would be decided.

The work was exhilarating. Bao went suddenly from being a director of an institute to one of the most influential men in China. In a country where each political declaration takes on key importance, it was he who shaped the premier's speeches, choosing the words publicly spoken by Zhao. Behind the closed doors of the Zhongnanhai compound, where members of the Chinese leadership lived and worked, Bao Tong designed the country's new political architecture. In this context, introducing true reforms was an extremely delicate undertaking. "All China," says Bao Tong "had been indoctrinated by Mao's thoughts. For thirty years, the Chinese had been taught to hate the market economy." Bao and Zhao now had to convince the Chinese of the opposite, that only a market economy could improve their lives. "What we did was de-Maoize the economy," Bao Tong tells me. Thus the words had to be chosen carefully. To speak of a market economy when the reforms were beginning would have put off too many people. During the 1980s, Zhao first presented his reforms as a kind of "autonomy," then spoke of "economic benefits." He sought terms that would be acceptable for the political forces that could derail the economic reforms. But all the terms, says Bao Tong, meant the same thing: a market economy.

As for political reforms, Bao Tong realized quite quickly that Deng Xiaoping did not intend to commit himself very far when it came to democratization. "It was Deng who proposed the discussion on the political system," Bao tells me twenty years later in his apartment. "But we all knew he didn't have radical changes in mind. He told us on at least three occasions we should not be inspired by the West in the reforms we were contemplating. He wanted to protect the party at all costs. It would have been intolerable for him if the Communist Party had lost power. When Deng spoke of political reforms, he mainly had in mind separating the Communist Party from the affairs of state, which would be entrusted to young professionals who could run the new economy according to the laws of the market, and not based on Marxist doctrine. More rational management of the state would reduce the arbitrariness of the Communist Party's decisions and renew the Chinese people's confidence in the party. But it was out of the question for him to cross the Rubicon of Western democracy, with its free elections in which several parties competed. That was why he stated his four cardinal principles, the last of which, the Communist Party's monopoly of power, was the cornerstone."

Zhao Ziyang and Hu Yaobang didn't know how far they could push democratization but tried by all possible means to convince Deng that China had to contemplate greater changes. They even spoke to him of American futurist Alvin Toffler and his bestseller, *The Third Wave*. In this book that would inspire more than a few politicians, Toffler maintains that most societies go from a first agricultural wave to a second industrial wave before engaging in a third post-industrial wave. Zhao and Hu believed that China could not let itself miss the boat of modernization predicted by Toffler. We don't know what Deng's reaction was to their exhortations, but it is interesting to note that Toffler concluded that progress could go backwards as much as it could go sideways or forward, depending on the society. After the Tiananmen Square massacre, the Communist regime would prove it was possible for China to ride on the wave of economic progress while letting the wave of democratic reform die on the shore.

At the beginning of the 1980s, however, things weren't that simple or clear. Deng launched China on a highway to modernization with one foot on the gas pedal of the economy and the other on the brakes of democracy. While he wanted the Chinese to take inspiration from NASA's scientific achievements, learn to build cars like Ford, and become used to the idea that foreigners could invest in new domestic enterprises, he certainly did not want the Chinese to embrace the American political model, which was to be avoided at all costs. Back from his triumphant tour of the United States, worried about the growing Democracy Wall movement, Deng launched a vast propaganda offensive in the official newspapers to warn the Chinese of the dangers and failures of liberal American society. On the one hand, scientific innovation and a business sense had perhaps allowed the Americans to rise in the ranks of economic powers, but on the other hand, their political system had produced only inequality. Long articles described how the rich lived behind closed doors in their luxurious apartments, fearful of being robbed by masses of the poor, the rejects of the American model. All one had to do was look in the shadows of the skyscrapers, the symbols of American success, one journalist wrote, to see the shortcomings of liberal society: misery, prostitution, and criminality. The American "democratic paradise," the Chinese press proclaimed in unison, was only a myth. Then the charge ended with the classic argument of Marxism versus liberal democracy. Because nothing differentiates the two big American political parties, the Republicans and the Democrats, American democracy is for all intents a one-party system where the bourgeoisie exploits the masses.[3]

Deng's approach may have seemed paradoxical, but his was only an apparent contradiction. He was telling the Chinese that while it was desirable for China to borrow a degree of economic freedom from the West, it was just as important for the Communist Party to protect them from the excesses of this freedom. Upholding the party dictatorship thus became a condition for the success of the economic U-turn Deng wanted for China. In an important speech he gave to Communist Party officials in 1980, Deng set out his core belief: "The Party," he declared, "cannot be separated from the people and the people cannot be separated from the Party." A multiple-party system, as some supporters of democracy were suggesting, would undermine the country's unity, he continued. Unless everyone accepted the Communist Party's leaders, Deng concluded, China would sink into division and confusion and be incapable of succeeding in its modernization.[4]

Deng Xiaoping's reasoning was not completely new. To some extent, it echoed the thinking of Chinese reformers, whether those of the self-strengthening movement of the end of the nineteenth century, the Hundred Days' Reform, or the Movement of May 4, 1919. All these reformers shared the belief that China should take from the West the finest of what it had to offer in terms of science and philosophy, not with a view to imitating the West but to better compete with powers such as England and Germany and resist their imperialism. Deng took this reasoning even further by asserting there was no contradiction between a market economy and a Communist political regime. A market economy led by the Communist Party, he argued, was more stable because it was not subject to elections that could change the government every four years. Deng's successors, Jiang Zemin and Hu Jintao, would refine this reasoning and turn it into a dogma. Those who thought the market economy in China would naturally lead to a liberal democracy were wrong. Capitalism was a necessary evil that would allow China to develop itself sufficiently to reach the objectives of socialism. In other words, it was only a stage in its development. From then on, anyone who argued in favour of China's democratization was guilty of wanting to usurp the Communist Party's power and prevent the country from progressing. This explains why, twenty years later, activists such as Hu Jia and Liu Xiaobo were sentenced to severe prison sentences simply for demanding democracy and the respect of rights on the Internet. Demanding another sort of democracy than that of the Communist Party was a kind of political heresy that was not tolerated, as we will see later.

While they denounced the faults and excesses of Western democracy, in the 1980s Chinese leaders still continued to promote the virtues of what they called socialist democracy. In their eyes, it was indispensable to China's economic modernization. It is important to understand that democracy, as conceived by Chinese leaders, is founded on a completely different, even contrary, principle than liberal democracy. In Western countries, it is understood that all citizens may exercise their rights to defend their private interests. In China, the opposite is true. Citizens must exercise their rights in the public interest. In his remarkable essay on Chinese democracy,

American sinologist Andrew Nathan writes: "The use of rights for self-seeking purposes cannot be part of their legitimate purpose, and may even be damaging if it undermines the ability of the state to channel citizens' energies in a unified direction."[5] This conception of each person's rights and duties, continues Nathan, goes back to the Confucian tradition of social harmony. Communist thinkers and leaders of the 1980s, he concludes, were therefore most sincere when they spoke of democracy. But it was a different democracy from the one people exercise in the West. It is a misunderstanding about the meaning of democracy that persists today more than ever.

According to Bao Tong, neither he nor Zhao Ziyang was satisfied with the direction the discussion on political reforms was taking at the end of the 1980s. But they had to be careful, as the conservative members of the politburo were still very influential and would use the slightest setback in the economic liberalization program to urge Deng Xiaoping to pull back from the reforms. "We were convinced that China had to give itself a truly democratic system," says Bao Tong, "but we were also very aware that it would be rejected if we proposed it in those terms. So we couched the idea of democracy in socialist vocabulary. We proposed developing a socialist democratic policy. If we had to dress up our project in socialist terms, we were ready to do so. We wanted to go as far as possible on the road of democratization, but didn't know how far we could go. At the very least, we needed to begin by reducing the Party's influence in the country's affairs." Deng sometimes leaned on the side of the reformers, who urged him to accelerate the reforms, and sometimes on the side of the conservatives, who wanted him to slow down. The situation was very fluid; reformers couldn't take anything for granted. "Deng had two sides," Bao Tong remembers. "He went back and forth like a pendulum. Sometimes he favoured the reforms, sometimes he asserted the four principles of socialism. He was both a sincere supporter of the reforms and a determined defender of the things we had to reform."

Deng's ambivalence is perhaps explained in part by the fact that the economic reforms were actually turning Chinese society upside down. Farmers suddenly had permission to sell the surplus of their crops; the directors of state-owned enterprises were encouraged to produce what they could sell rather than quotas set arbitrarily by the party; governors of provinces were granted greater autonomy. They were even asked to court foreign investors. Any Chinese who wanted to could go into business by opening a stand on a street corner. These changes challenged traditional relationships within Chinese society. Young people were discovering Western fashion and music, to the great displeasure of their parents; the generation gap, that American concept of the 1960s, was making its appearance in China. With his economic modernization, Deng Xiaoping had unintentionally opened the door of the Chinese fortress to the Trojan Horse of individualism. This would not be without consequence.

Ironically, two of the main shortcomings for which Chinese propaganda criticized American society, inequality and corruption, did not take long to appear in China. Deng's model of a *market economy for the public good led by a socialist democracy* did not support the weight of its contradictions for very long. Encouraged to work for profit, the Chinese naturally took care of their private interests. The lure of making a profit won out over the collective good. Rapidly, two classes emerged: the people who profited from the new economy and the others, who didn't have the means or the imagination to do so. The frustration many Chinese felt doubled as a feeling of injustice when they realized a majority of the newly rich were party officials or members of their families. Leaders of government enterprises, in particular, were eager to display the wealth they were accumulating from public funds. They bought themselves foreign luxury cars, treated themselves to trips, and gave lavish dinners where influence peddling was common. A survey at the time revealed that more than 80 per cent of Chinese who lived in cities believed that a majority of party officials were corrupt. Incredibly, in the same survey, 63 per cent of these officials admitted to being involved in some form of corruption.[6] Deng's reforms, whose aim was to renew the party's credibility, were actually undermining it further.

The popular discontent was a double-edged sword for Zhao Ziyang and Bao Tong. On the one hand, this criticism, expressed as rarely before, allowed Zhao and other reformers to argue for greater liberalization. It was proof, they said, that the regime had to be more open to discussion and better able to channel dissent. On the other hand, it provided ammunition to opponents of the reforms who were trying to convince Deng Xiaoping to backtrack. They claimed liberalization was a failure and that people didn't want it. Corruption, inequality, and inflation, which the government had trouble controlling, were presented as direct consequences of the economic reforms. The debate gave way to numerous intrigues in the apartments and corridors of the Zhongnanhai Compound. Deng, like a sphinx, rarely revealed his hand; he let the factions compete with one another before making a decision. Zhao Ziyang and Bao Tong quickly understood they had to build support outside the government if they hoped to move their plans for democratization forward. They turned to the intellectuals.

At the beginning of the 1980s, Chinese intellectuals enjoyed incredible freedom of speech and movement. It was as if Chinese society were undergoing such an explosion with the liberalization of the economy that authorities were less aware or had less time to crack down on intellectuals who criticized them. For reformers inside the government, no support was more precious than that of activists of Wang Juntao's calibre. Wang was one of China's rising intellectual stars. The independent research institute he ran with his colleague Chen Zeming as well as their journal on political analysis made them essential allies of Bao Tong. Bao consulted them regularly and used their writings to stimulate thinking within his reform committee. Wang had become a celebrity of sorts at the age of sixteen, after he was arrested during the demonstrations following Zhou Enlai's death. Wang was not a martyr, like another famous dissident Wei Jingsheng, who rotted in prison for calling Deng Xiaoping a dictator. He was a moderate, a pragmatist, who wanted to reform the political regime rather than overthrow it.

Wang had an acute sense of how to use his contacts and notoriety. One evening in 1979, accompanied by a friend, he even dared knock at the home of the party general secretary, Hu Yaobang, the man Deng put in charge of reforming the Communist Party and making the government more democratic. Even though he was scarcely twenty years old, Wang was well known. The guards did not try to intercept him, and Hu invited him in, even though his visit was unannounced. "Hu," Wang said, "knew me well. He had read all the issues of our political magazine *Beijing Spring*. He was very grateful that at our demonstration on April 5, 1976, we supported him, Deng, and the other party leaders who had been persecuted during the Cultural Revolution." Hu was a small man who gestured a lot when he spoke. That evening, he was worried about the direction of his reforms. "Hu told me: 'We want to carry out reforms, but how to proceed,'" Wang remembers. "'How do we make the transition?' he asked. 'How do we overcome the conservatives?' Then he asked me to tell him concretely what worked and what didn't work in the system. I suddenly realized we had a general idea of democracy, but no notion of what it meant in reality." That moment was a kind of epiphany for Wang. He left Hu's home firmly intending to build a framework for his ideas of reform. Less than ten years later, Wang was at the centre of the debate on reform in China.

Bao Tong and the reformers in the government not only consulted the intellectuals but also counted on them to promote publicly the idea of reform. The strategy was all the more effective because many of them were members of the Communist Party. One of the most popular was Fang Lizhi, an astrophysicist who was also vice-president of a university. He was nicknamed the Andrei Sakharov of China partly because, like the famous Soviet dissident, he was a scientist, but also because he dared criticize the regime openly. Fang toured Chinese universities, where he told students they had a role to play in reforming their country. The democracy they had to build, he told them, was part of each citizen's rights. Those rights, he said, were not "given by the top leaders of the nation. All people are born with them."[7] Lizhi was finally expelled from the party, a rather gentle sanction considering his statements. Had he made the same remarks a few years previous or today, he surely would have faced a prison sentence.

Despite the warnings of some members of the Communist leadership against the temptation of American freedom, or of freedom as a whole, the party found itself overtaken by intellectuals. Some, like journalist Liu Binyan, became a crusader against corruption in Communist ranks. Liu's credibility and Communist pedigree were beyond reproach. He was a revolutionary who fought the Japanese and the Kuomintang in Mao's army. As a journalist, he spent his life defending ordinary Chinese who were crushed by the government machinery, which earned him years in prison and in labour camps.[8] The fact that he was a party member and wrote in the official press gave him significant influence in righting the wrongs of party officials. He was so well known that people submitted their grievances to him rather than to the party. Liu had another ace up his sleeve: he had the ear of the general secretary and reformer, Hu Yaobang. Sometimes, rather than publishing a controversial article, he sent the file to Hu, who used it to punish the culprits internally.

Democracy activists in the 1980s had an advantage that those before them did not: the protection and patronage of the senior leaders of the Chinese government. Many historians compare this period following Mao's death to the Hundred Days' Reform of the young Guangxu Emperor at the end of the nineteenth century. The emperor, newly installed on the throne, had allied himself with reformers outside the court to modernize China and begin a transition to a constitutional monarchy, but Empress Cixi, who had acted for several years as her nephew's regent, had him arrested, putting an end to his ideas of reform, and took power until her death. As in Cixi's court, Communist leadership under Deng was divided into a reform wing and a conservative wing. When the events of Tiananmen Square disrupted the fragile framework of the reform, Deng did not hesitate to sacrifice Zhao Ziyang, as Cixi had sacrificed her nephew, scrapping his plans for political modernization.

From the mid-1980s on, the friction between the reformist and conservative wings was similar to that of two tectonic plates. Exasperated that intellectuals could attack the party's integrity and legitimacy with complete impunity, members of the party's old guard mobilized for a counteroffensive. On December 27, 1986, five veterans of the conservative wing, Wang Zhen, Peng Zhen, Hu Qiaomu, Bo Yibo, and Den Liqun, showed up at Deng's home. They asked him to fire Hu Yaobang, the party's general secretary and figurehead of the reforms. Hundreds of thousands of students had been holding sporadic protests in about thirty cities in China since November to denounce corruption and demand democracy. The elders held Hu personally responsible for this turmoil. Everything about Hu offended the conservatives. He liked suits and ties and even suggested replacing chopsticks, which to him smacked of feudalism, with the forks used in the West. Deng did not want to sacrifice his economic modernization program but shared the elders' exasperation at the avalanche of criticism being levelled at the Communist Party. He listened to them but reserved his decision. Certainly, Hu was beginning to irritate him deeply not only because he seemed to encourage intellectuals to attack the party but also because he already saw himself as Deng's successor. Deng was especially irritated by an interview Hu gave to a Hong Kong journalist in which he speculated about the patriarch's possible departure. Yet Hu was an old friend of Deng. They had fought the revolution together and regularly played bridge. And Deng did see him as his successor, even though he resented Hu speculating about it. Deep down, however, Deng was also aware that Hu carried too much political baggage. He came to the conclusion that he had to sacrifice him. On December 30, Deng convened a small group of those close to him, including Hu and Zhao. He was in a foul mood, and especially angry at Hu and Zhao for not having fought with more conviction the wave of "bourgeois liberalization" that accompanied economic liberalization. Modernization, he told them, needed leadership and "dictatorial measures" if necessary. Bourgeois liberalization, he concluded, would bring only turmoil.[9]

Hu Yaobang knew his days were numbered. Three days later, he handed in his resignation letter to Deng, in which he admitted to having made serious errors. According to those close to him, he later regretted not defending himself more. On January 16, Deng convened the seventeen members of the enlarged politburo to decide his fate. Most of them took turns to condemn Hu. Even Zhao Ziyang, his reformist comrade-in-arms, did not come to his defence. That same evening, state television announced Hu's departure. He was accused of not fighting "spiritual contamination" hard enough and encouraging "complete Westernization" as well as a "consumer society." The party's contradictions were laid out for all to see. Ironically, Zhao Ziyang came out the big winner in the firing of Hu Yaobang. He replaced him as party general secretary. It showed that while Deng had agreed to sacrifice Hu in the name of reinforcing discipline, he did not intend to sabotage his economic modernization. Zhao, aware of the context, played the game and tried to buy time. In front of more than two hundred party officials he criticized Hu, said he had been too "timid" in fighting against liberalism, and deemed that his resignation was justified. At the same time, he warned them he would not neglect economic liberalization. To make them understand that China would not turn back, he announced, they would remove the portraits of Marx, Engels, Lenin, and Stalin from Tiananmen Square.

While Hu Yaobang's departure placated the old guard, it did not put an end to the social tensions or the people's discontent; quite the contrary. Inflation was reaching new heights: in the space of three months, the price of fruit and vegetables increased by 50 per cent in Beijing. Hundreds of thousands of workers were laid off as soon as dying state-owned enterprises, which had formerly been immune from economic reality, had to function according to the rules of the market. Many of them simply did not survive the transition. In these conditions, the underground economy and corruption flourished. The government, in an effort to improve its image, fired one hundred and fifty thousand party members accused of being involved in the corruption. However, this measure seemed to have the opposite effect: for many Chinese, it revealed the extent of the corruption rather than an imminent end to it.

From that moment on, Zhao Ziyang came to realize the political changes would have to be bolder, and much more radical and daring, if the party hoped to maintain its relevance and credibility. Until then, Zhao had been mainly concerned with economic modernization, which he considered separate from political reform. But all that would change. "It was not until 1985 or 1986 that my understanding started to change," Zhao Ziyang said later. "My attention was aroused somewhat by events in the broader international environment and problems that had emerged in the Eastern bloc. Yet the main reason for the change was that I had come to see a need for political reform from the perspective of economic reform."[10] In other words, Zhao Ziyang realized his economic modernization would not be successful unless it was accompanied by deep political reform.

These revelations come from sound recordings Zhao produced in the early 2000s while under house arrest in Beijing. He recorded everything on about thirty mini-cassettes that he gave to a few of his friends, who had them smuggled out of China. This legacy of Zhao from beyond the grave, published in the spring of 2009, four years after his death, unveils his true intentions and thinking. The recordings were published in book form in Hong Kong under the title *Prisoner of the State: The Secret Journal of Premier Zhao Ziyang*. The publisher was Bao Bu, the son of Bao Tong, the disgraced former right-hand man of Zhao Ziyang. Bao Tong secretly participated in the project, even though he was under constant police surveillance. He even wrote the preface to the Chinese edition of the book. The document is a major source of embarrassment for the Chinese government, as it reveals what happened in Deng Xiaoping's entourage during crucial moments in the Tiananmen crisis. Needless to say, the book is banned in China. In June 2009, Customs officers even searched the luggage of travellers arriving from Hong Kong to make sure they weren't trying to smuggle it into the mainland.

In the recordings, Zhao explains in detail for the first time how far he was ready to go to reform the political machinery. "Of course, the political reform I had in mind for China at the time, up until 1989, was not an adaptation of a multi-party system or the implementation of a Western-style parliamentary system," specifies Zhao from the start. "Nor did I think that the Communist Party's ruling position should change."[11] But if the "party's ruling status need not be changed," according to Zhao, "the way it governed" had to change radically. And that imperatively required establishing rule of law, without which the market economy could not function and develop. In 1987, Zhao drew up a list of changes he deemed necessary to achieve

this. First, explained Zhao, they had to increase transparency in the party
and in decision making. In the USSR, Gorbachev called this opening
"glasnost." For us, Zhao said, this would be transparency. "This would have
changed the long-standing 'black-box operation,' where the public is only
given the final result of a decision. As soon as the government announced
a decision, it moved on to implementation, but people were not privy to
the process by which the decision had been made. This is very important.
People have the right to know."[12] Not only did he want the Chinese to be
more aware of the way the party reached its decisions, but he also thought
they needed to be consulted more before deciding. To do so, the government
had to establish channels of communication and consultation with the various
groups in society. But first it had to legalize the existence of unions, chambers
of commerce, and women's and student groups outside the party framework,
which was not permitted at the time.

Zhao believed that while the government had to consult the people
more, the Communist Party needed to look more democratic. From that
point on, he thought of increasing the number of candidates for positions
in the party. "Even though we could not all at once adopt the methods of
Western-style elections," said Zhao, "the Communist Party could at least
increase the number of proposed candidates, including for positions such
as chairman of the NPC or the premier of the State Council. With more
candidates, the people would have a real choice."[13] Zhao even contemplated
allowing other political parties to take part in the deliberations of the People's
Congress, the Chinese parliament that met once a year to ratify the
government's decisions. At the time of the founding of the People's Republic,
Mao had actually introduced eight secondary parties, including the
Democratic Party of China. Until then, however, these had only been
"decorative vases" with no political influence as they had to accept the
supervision of the Communist Party. To complete the political modernization
he contemplated, Zhao believed the Communist Party's exercise of power
had to contain two fundamental principles. The first was to replace rule by
men with rule of law. "We needed to protect citizens' rights in concrete

terms," Zhao explains in his memoirs. "This was extremely important. Our constitution was a good one, but there were no laws in place to support its implementation." Finally, Zhao was convinced that this new, more open, more transparent, more democratic political system had to function in the context of greater press freedom.[14]

In the winter of 1987, as the new general secretary of the party, Zhao Ziyang was the most powerful man after Deng Xiaoping. He was thus in an ideal position to advance his ideas of political reform. The 13th Congress of the Party, scheduled for the fall, was the perfect opportunity for adopting the new political structure he had in mind. But Zhao knew very well that for the more conservative members of the Politburo what he contemplated was heresy, even betrayal. So he avoided showing his hand. He asked Bao Tong to get to work at writing proposals for reform that would be submitted to thousands of delegates at the party congress. It was a delicate task. "Of course," says Zhao, "in these texts, some of the ideas could not be expressed as explicitly and some could not be included at all."[15] This led Bao Tong, in his own words, to "give the modernization project a socialist aspect." Today, considering the disaster that the Tiananmen Square crisis represented for China's democratization, Bao regretted that he and Zhao had not begun pushing these reforms earlier. "We should have started them in the early 1980s," he tells me.

Zhao Ziyang's caution and pragmatism are explained by the fact that he knew Deng was fiercely opposed to any reform that would dilute the party's power or that even slightly resembled what was happening in Western countries. "What Deng had in mind for political reforms was different from what most people understood by that: the modernization of the state and democratization." Zhao maintains that "Deng was particularly opposed to a multi-party system, tripartite separation of powers, and the parliamentary system of Western nations—and firmly rejected them." At the time when Zhao, with the help of Bao Tong, drafted the principal discussion papers to be submitted to the 13th Congress of the Party, Deng, he writes, warned him on several occasions that "the idea of political reform absolutely must not be influenced by Western parliamentarian political ideas. Let there not be even a trace of it!"[16]

In this context, Zhao was not in a position to submit his entire political modernization to the Congress of the Party. He and Bao Tong still tried to have measures adopted to distance the Communist Party further from management of government affairs. More positions would be subject to internal elections and the mandate of various party officers would be limited. The 13th Congress of the Party, which took place in the fall of 1987 in Beijing, also heralded a change of generation in those holding power. No less than nine veterans of the politburo announced their retirement, including Deng Xiaoping, as well as some of the fiercest opponents of the economic modernization program. If there were doubts about the changing of the guard, they disappeared quickly when the new Central Committee appeared before the international press in suits and ties instead of the cotton tunic of the revolutionary era. When a foreign journalist mentioned the striped suit worn by Zhao, the regime's new strongman, Zhao smiled widely and showed him the "made in China" label on the back of the jacket: a very fitting metaphor for the times.

Zhao Ziyang perhaps felt that time was on his side. His relationship with Deng was excellent. There was nothing to foretell the fateful moment that less than two years later would lead to his downfall—Deng's decision to bring in the army to quell the student movement in Tiananmen Square. Deng even confided to Zhao that he saw him as the general secretary of the party for another two terms. At the party congress, Zhao, to Deng's great satisfaction, also managed to resolve one of the philosophical contradictions of the transition to a market economy. The apparent contradiction of the Communist Party overseeing capitalism, and its inability to explain it, was annoying for party leaders. Zhao Ziyang's solution was both elegant and simple. The capitalism of the 1980s, Zhao explained to congress, was not an end in itself or a final destination for China. It was only an "initial stage of socialism" that would end up being made obsolete with the completion of socialism. This new precept, which still applies today, had the advantage of stripping Zhao's opponents of their ammunition in opposing economic modernization.

Confident with his new position, Zhao Ziyang accelerated the economic modernization process and began implementing political reforms. In his opinion, the two were now inseparable. Bao Tong, who since the fall of 1986 had been in charge of the committee that explored the means of political reform, increased consultations with intellectuals and other political activists. Some of Zhao's allies, however, didn't share his optimism. They believed Zhao had to dilute too many of his proposals at the party congress and feared he would not be able to overcome the conservatives' opposition. These intellectuals knew China's history well and were very aware of the fragility, even the danger, of their undertaking. Bao Tong later said he felt as if he were "riding a tiger." In addition, some of the intellectuals concluded that to ensure the passage to democracy, Zhao Ziyang, after succeeding Deng, had to introduce a period of "new authoritarianism" to impose his political reforms upon his detractors. Wang Juntao, although he was a democrat, briefly supported this option. Wang and other intellectuals concluded that the reforms were getting bogged down, slowed down from inside the regime by conservative elements, and that only a new leader with increased powers could make them triumph. That was the sign that, in certain respects, China had changed very little in seventy years. Many democrats, like Sun Yat-sen before them, were convinced that only an enlightened dictator could guarantee the success of the democratization. The theory of new authoritarianism had been developed by American political scientist Samuel Huntington from Harvard. Based on the examples of Singapore and South Korea, he postulated that a period of strong centralism is sometimes needed to overcome bureaucratic resistance during a period of reform. Zhao had made the proposal to Deng. The modernization of a country such as China had to go through a period during which authoritarian leaders are the driving force of change, he explained to the patriarch. According to Zhao, Deng said he agreed with this notion, adding that the terms needed to be refined. Yet the idea failed long before it could be put to the test. Zhao felt that at the very least he needed more power to carry through his reforms. He would like to have led both the government and the party and had told Deng as much. Deng, says Zhao in his memoirs, was not opposed, but never followed through on it either.

Zhao's position, however, was more precarious than it seems. Even though he had quit the politburo and did not have an official position in the Chinese leadership, Deng Xiaoping still remained the regime's supreme authority. The patriarch also gave himself the means to intervene if necessary by secretly creating a central advisory committee made up of elders who, like him, reserved the right to supervise new government leaders. Creating this committee was technically unconstitutional, as it was never put to a vote. But that didn't matter. The power was still in Deng's hands. This committee would ultimately allow Deng to order military intervention against the students during the Tiananmen Square protest. The elders had an additional advantage in Li Peng, a hardline partisan like themselves, whom they had appointed premier. Li Peng worked relentlessly to thwart Zhao Ziyang's plans for reform. He was also the main insider responsible for the regime's tough stance against the students.

As of 1988, Zhao Ziyang's authority was being undermined by the failure of his economic modernization program. Despite all its efforts, the government could not control inflation. On campuses, students demonstrated against the high cost of living as much as for democracy. Besieged on all sides, the government decided to liberalize prices. The Chinese rushed to the stores to stock up on all they could before price control was abolished. The step turned out to be a fiasco, and Zhao had to take responsibility. From that moment on, his authority was no longer the same, and his halo as a reformer was forever tarnished. He was required to participate in a self-criticism session before the politburo and the state council. The conservatives in the government sensed the tide had turned. In late 1988, one of their leaders, Chen Yun, even attacked him publicly, accusing him on behalf of others of allowing bourgeois ideologies to dominate the political landscape. Then three of the elders, Bo Yibo, Wang Zhen, and Li Xiannian, asked Deng Xiaoping to force Zhao to resign at the party plenum in March. Deng refused, saying he had already sacrificed a general secretary, Hu Yaobang, and that there was no obvious replacement for Zhao.

Amid this uncertainty and political intrigue, Hu Yaobang suffered a heart attack during a politburo meeting on the morning of April 8, 1989. He died a week later. The old hand at politics, stripped of power and influence since his dismissal two years earlier, was to become a more powerful agent of change after his death than during his lifetime. On April 17, more than ten thousand students converged on Tiananmen Square to pay homage to him. This was an indirect way of expressing their fear that the conservative wing of the party was thwarting the promised reforms. Zhao Ziyang, whose influence was diminishing, saw the student protests as an opportunity to revive his reforms, especially those aimed at democratization. "I also felt that if the student demonstrations could be resolved along the principles of democracy and law, through dialogue and an easing of tensions, it could possibly boost China's reform, including political reform."[17] History decided otherwise. Tiananmen was the prelude to his personal and political downfall. For the six weeks this unprecedented rebellion lasted, Zhao increased efforts to resolve the crisis but was constantly neutralized by Premier Li Peng. Bao Tong, meanwhile, ensured the liaison between the reform wing of the government and the student leaders. He would pay dearly for it. Bao and Zhao had sided with the students. They would have to drink from the poisoned chalice of democratization.

6
Wang Dan's Shooting Star

London, January 2009

Wang Dan arranged to meet me in a café across from the British Museum. He is the symbol of the Tiananmen Square movement, the young Beijing University history student who shook the Communist regime. He now lives in California but is spending the winter of 2009 in London thanks to a scholarship from Oxford University. Veterans of the Tiananmen Square student movement still enjoy a certain market value with elite Western universities. Yet Wang Dan seems to tire of this role. Wang Juntao had to intervene on my behalf from New York for Wang to respond to my emails. I have the impression that he agreed to talk to me more out of duty than because he really wants to.

When I come out of the subway station, brilliant sunshine is melting away what is left of a rare snowfall that paralyzed the British capital for two days. The cold has misted over the windows of the café, making the place look darker. Once inside, it takes me a few moments to realize that Wang Dan is seated at the first table, very close to the entrance. He is the kind of person who would not necessarily be noticeable in a crowd. He no longer wears glasses but at forty still looks like a teenager. His physique and unassuming appearance seem to contradict his place in history. I told him I wanted to talk more about China's future than the past, even if this is only partly true. I believe that is why he finally accepted my invitation. I offer him coffee, but he doesn't want anything.

This first contact is not easy, especially since I have trouble working the tape recorder I've just bought and it takes me three tries to start it properly. Yet during the interview, I conclude that the distance I first sensed in Wang Dan arises from his natural reserve. This is not unusual: many orators are very shy. But I also feel that the man before me is wounded. As much as the role he played in the events of Tiananmen Square made him famous, the escape, prison, and exile that followed seem to have broken something essential in him. He tells me that, contrary to other dissidents, he refuses to be defined by Tiananmen Square, to be a prisoner of the past. "Once a week, I like to go dancing," he adds, as if to prove there is a life beyond dissidence. These days he is trying to have his doctoral thesis published to earn a position in a university, preferably in Taiwan, he explains, which would allow him to be closer to mainland China. For he still hopes to return home, not to revive the struggle for democracy but simply to live there and see his relatives and friends. It would take only a gesture from the government, the granting of a kind of immunity, but clearing the names of the veterans of Tiananmen Square and allowing them to return to China is a step the Communist leaders refuse to take. Even though I promised to talk more about the future than the past, I realize that what defines Wang Dan is mostly the past. He knows it too. The discussion warms up, like the London air the day after the snowfall.

Beijing, April 27, 1989

Wang Dan was excited. With another student leader, Shen Tong, he summoned universities to a march that could well herald either the triumph or the end of the student movement. On this April morning, they wondered if it was better to cancel the march or forge ahead, regardless of the consequences. The decision was both difficult and crucial. The previous day, April 26, the *People's Daily* published a scathing editorial in which it described the student protests as a conspiracy aiming to challenge the leadership of the Communist Party, a sign that the government had just adopted a hard-line approach. No one knew how far the authorities were ready to go to quell the student demonstrations. "Under the banner of democracy," accused the editorial inspired partly by Deng Xiaoping himself, "they are trying to destroy the legal and democratic system. Their goal is to poison the people's minds, create turmoil throughout the country, and destroy political stability and unity." Wang Dan and other student leaders were dismayed by the editorial. In their innocence, they had taken to the streets to support the reformist elements in the government, not to overthrow the Communist Party.

The editorial, however, changed everything. If they did not respond forcefully, that would be the end of their movement and their demands for reform. But if they rose to the bait of the provocative editorial, they were liable to transform their request for dialogue into a confrontation with the government. In the circumstances, Wang and Shen didn't know how many people would agree to march. Above all they feared that many students would be intimidated by the government's threats. Already, certain universities were announcing they would not take part in the march. Tens of thousands of police officers were brought in to the capital as reinforcements and stationed in the area surrounding the campuses. To minimize confrontation, Wang and Shen decided that the march would stop at the Third Ring Road; they would not force matters by going all the way to Tiananmen Square. Wang Dan, a young history student with big glasses framing his cherubic face, who knew how to stir up crowds, was no longer sure of himself. A few days earlier, during the founding meeting of the movement, he had declared, perhaps a little too recklessly: "We will take back democracy and freedom from the old men who stole power from us!" Suddenly, however, Wang and Shen felt uneasy. Actions, more than words, had consequences, and they hesitated to launch the students into a march where they would have to come up against police barricades. This was an enormous responsibility.

To some extent the decision was made for them. More than eight thousand students, furious at the editorial in the *People's Daily*, showed up for the march. They didn't like in the least that the regime claimed they were being manipulated by a small number of agitators. Some of them were ready to accept the most severe consequences for their actions. They shaved their heads and wrote wills to the attention of their parents in case they were killed there. Shortly before nine o'clock in the morning, the procession, carried by what students considered to be destiny, began to march. They chanted slogans for democracy; those in the French department waved a large banner on which they wrote: "Vive la liberté!" (Long live freedom!). The demonstrators, however, had scarcely covered a few hundred metres when they reached a first barrier. Three rows of police officers blocked their way. Wang Dan and Shen Tong went to speak to an officer, an older man. "You know you can't stop us," they told him. "Why don't you let us pass? We are only going to Third Ring Road and then turning back. If you don't let us pass, we're going to rush your line, and after that none of us will be able to control the students."[1] The police officer did not answer but ordered his men to move aside. Wang and Shen looked at each other and smiled. They never thought it would be so easy.

It would not have been so easy had it not been for the head of security, Qiao Shi, who wanted to avoid any violence against the students. Qiao, whose daughter studied in Texas, did not want to take responsibility for firing at the demonstrators. That is why he ordered his men to block their way without using batons or weapons, hoping that would be enough to dissuade them from marching. Once they had crossed the first barrier, however, the students, Wang Dan and Shen Tong in the lead, no longer intended to stop. They would march all the way to Tiananmen Square, twelve kilometres away. One by one, the police barriers opened before them like the sea parting for Moses. With each kilometre, the crowd grew. Not only did students from other universities join the march, but there were also workers who left their factories, teachers who abandoned their classrooms, and ordinary people who sensed something unique was happening. They all shared the same grievances: inflation, corruption, the growing gap between the newly rich and the others, and the certainty that the government had to change its way and become more open, more transparent, more willing to listen to Chinese like themselves. Newsstand owners came out into the street to give the students free drinks and grandmothers threw provisions to them from their balconies. When the procession arrived close to Tiananmen Square several hours later, it contained hundreds of thousands of people. Thus civilian China was saying no to its government when it asked them to condemn the youth rebellion. Wang Dan, who a few hours earlier had hesitated to confront the Communist regime, suddenly became the unlikely symbol of the struggle for democracy, a puny David before an aging Goliath. On that afternoon in April 1989, everything seemed possible.

Chinese university campuses in the mid-1980s had something of the atmosphere of May 1968 in Paris. The students' traditional conformity was giving way to a questioning of the established order and an idealism rarely seen in China. Deng Xiaoping's modernizations allowed thousands of Chinese youth to study abroad. They brought back new ideas but also critical thinking that was a distinctive feature of foreign universities. The status quo they were challenging, however, was very different from the one prevailing in the West. While from Berkeley to the Sorbonne, protesters quoted Marx, calling for a more just and egalitarian society, the young Chinese were inspired by the freedom of speech they saw abroad and called for the end of Marxist orthodoxy. But there was more. The Communist world itself was in crisis. In Poland, Lech Walesa and the Solidarity Movement were shaking the pillars of the Communist regime. In Moscow, Mikhail Gorbachev tried to save the USSR from collapse by two major reforms, perestroika and glasnost. The Communist universe was wavering.

Inspired by what they saw in Warsaw and Moscow, the young Chinese also called for changes. In universities, they organized discussion groups and conferences where they debated reform and democracy. When they spoke of transparency, they used the Chinese term *toumingdu*, a direct translation of glasnost. Any speaker deemed too timid in his criticisms of the system was booed or sometimes even expelled from the platform. As a young history student at Beijing University, Wang Dan was right in the hub of this reflection and questioning. He participated regularly in a discussion group, the Wednesday Forum, before founding his own Democracy Salon, where he invited speakers to address the students. Back then, Wang had a head start over many of the students. Since his mother worked in the archives, he had access to foreign books and magazines. Moreover, both his parents were graduates of Beijing University. The family had a long association with the famous university. Yet Wang Dan says he still didn't have "a clear idea of what democratic reforms we wanted then, but we were certain of one thing: we wanted more freedom."

Many students were spending more time in salons and cafés than in classrooms. They would often gather at the foot of a statue of Cervantes located on what they called the "Democracy Lawn." If there was a certain irony in the fact that the students were preparing to launch an assault on the Communist regime in the shadow of a bronze statue of the author of *Don Quixote*, it went largely unnoticed in the excitement of this spring of protest. In those days of April 1989, who could have predicted that the Chinese students' spontaneous momentum toward Tiananmen Square, at the time of reformer Hu Yaobang's death, would trigger such a political maelstrom, that in only a few weeks the student movement would become a threat to the Chinese Communist Party's survival and that its leaders would pay so dearly for their actions?

The student movement was the driving force of a deep desire for change in Chinese society due to a unique convergence of circumstances in the second half of the 1980s. When they reopened the universities after the dark period of the Cultural Revolution, Chinese leaders encouraged masses of young people to pursue graduate studies, thereby promoting the role of the intellectual. In 1977, China had only four hundred universities; in 1988, it had more than a thousand, seventy of which were in Beijing. At the end of the 1980s a university opened in China every three or four days! Many students were encouraged to study sociology, philosophy, or history to become the thinkers of tomorrow. Yet practically overnight, Deng Xiaoping, with his four modernizations, minimized the importance of these new intellectuals to promote the new entrepreneurs. Suddenly, graduates in social sciences, promised they would become the new Chinese elite, had trouble finding work. Many ended up as salespeople or hotel employees. Any newsstand owner without a degree earned more money than someone with a doctorate!

In his analysis of the Tiananmen student movement, sociologist Dingxin Zhao of the University of Chicago observed that Chinese students did not understand much about the new capitalism. They believed the new market economy would make them richer; they never thought it would degrade the prestige and privileges of intellectuals. This discrepancy, Dingxin argued, was a major source of grievance that fuelled the Tiananmen student movement.[2] But there is more. Many students who hoped to complete their studies abroad were told by the government that China no longer had the means due to fluctuations in its new economy. Chinese leaders were also irritated that the scholarships they were giving students to study abroad were becoming passes for emigration. Very few students who won scholarships to foreign universities actually came back to live and work in China. According to a joke at the time, there were two categories of students in Chinese universities: the Tuo, who were studying for English exams to go abroad, and the Ma, who spent their times in cafés playing mah-jong.

The students also shared many of the frustrations of other Chinese at what they perceived as the injustices of economic liberalization. This was not without consequences. When they denounced corruption and inequality and demanded more of a say in the country's affairs, Chinese students were actually expressing the same grievances as their parents. Today we know that Communist leaders were very aware that the students' demands went beyond an expression of youthful frustration. A survey carried out for the Party's Central Committee in March 1989, scarcely a few weeks before the occupation of Tiananmen Square, reveals a high level of support for the student protests among the population. More than 50 per cent of adults surveyed believed it was legitimate for the students to take to the streets to assert their grievances; only 12 per cent thought otherwise. The survey, prepared by the Communist Youth League, concluded that this "similarity of attitudes between young people and adults should be a major concern."[3] In their report to the Central Committee, the survey authors reported other disturbing tendencies among the students, many of whom believed communism was a utopia that would never be realized. More than half did not want to become members of the Communist Party. Sixty per cent felt China's modernization should not follow the socialist path. This amounted to a total repudiation of the Communist regime and its program. The authors of the report talked about what they called the students' growing tendency to be "politically confused" and espouse "wrong views." But while the Communist Party was very clear as to the grievances of the Chinese youth, it could not admit that its policies were the cause. The authors of the report concluded that the students were manipulated by a few agitators, including the disciples of Wei Jingsheng, one of the leaders of the 1978 Democracy Wall movement who had been rotting in prison for ten years, and infiltration by foreign powers.[4]

The people's discontent was all the more worrisome for the regime in that it occurred at the beginning of what was supposed to be an important year for China, as 1989 was actually the seventieth anniversary of the May Fourth Movement. In 1919, thousands of students had besieged Tiananmen Square to show their discontent at China's humiliation during the Treaty of Versailles and to demand democracy. They deemed it was the only way to strengthen China and allow it to defend itself against Western imperialism. Since then, May 4 has become as important an anniversary for the Chinese as the storming of the Bastille is for the French. In 1989, the Chinese government planned to organize big celebrations for May 4, which would perhaps allow the Chinese to unite around an important patriotic anniversary and have them forget their grievances. The students were also preparing to commemorate May 4. But they saw themselves as carrying the legacy of the students of 1919, not as allies of the government. Many were also inspired by the two hundredth anniversary of the French Revolution, for which Mao and the Chinese Communist imagination had always had an affinity. In early April, Wang Dan, accompanied by other Beijing University students, wrote an open letter to the authorities, asking them to honour the spirit of May 4 by allowing more freedom of speech. Wang reminded them it was from this same university, this "birthplace of this extraordinary movement of democratic enlightenment," that the students had left in 1919 to go protest in Tiananmen Square.[5]

The government and the students were not alone in wanting to take advantage of May 4 to advance their cause. Wang Juntao and other veterans of the Democracy Wall saw in it the opportunity to give new momentum to the political reforms that had languished since the conservatives managed to undermine Zhao Ziyang's authority. The veterans of the Democracy Wall met, as of December 1988, in a suite that Wang Juntao and Chen Zeming rented in State Council's Number 2 Guest Hostel, near the Beijing Zoo. A good part of the Chinese intellectual jet set joined Wang and Chen's initiative. There was Fang Lizhi, who was expelled from the party for the critical lectures he gave university students; Ren Wanding, a friend of Wei Jingsheng, who spent four years in prison before founding the China Human Rights League; and Zhang Gang, a former Red Guard who was Bao Tong's right-hand man in the government's reform committee. One of the group's first actions was to write Deng Xiaoping on the eve of the May 4 celebrations to call for the release of political prisoners, including Wei Jingsheng, China's notorious dissident. They also formed a committee to investigate the conditions of these detainees, which they called Amnesty 89.[6] When the government rejected their request, they responded with new petitions, which more and more intellectuals agreed to sign.

At the time, Fang Lizhi was at the centre of a diplomatic controversy during American President George Bush's visit to Beijing. American Ambassador Winston Lord included Fang Lizhi on the guest list for the banquet Bush was to give for his Chinese hosts in one of Beijing's only Western hotels, the Sheraton Great Wall. Furious, Chinese authorities threatened to boycott the dinner if Fang attended. The Americans agreed to seat Fang in the back of the room and avoid any public contact with the president. But on February 28, the day of the reception, the police prevented

Fang and his wife from reaching the hotel. The incident marred Bush's visit. The American president still gave a pair of cowboy boots to Premier Li Peng, who in turn presented him with two bicycles.[7] The affair nevertheless revealed how much the American government was aware of divisions in Chinese society and seemed ready through symbolic gestures to support the reformers.

Wang, Chen, and other intellectuals were aware that fundamental forces had just been set in motion in Chinese society. They saw in them the opportunity to take a leading role. The civil society they imagined as a counterbalance to the Communist Party was taking shape in student groups, in the voices of protest that arose in the population, even among entrepreneurs, who demanded new rights such as the right to own property. In the eyes of Wang Juntao and Chen Zeming, the intellectuals, who traditionally worked in isolation, cut off from the people, had a new role to play. They had to organize the population in a huge political movement.[8] While for the moment most intellectuals still hoped to reform the regime from the inside, their movement could nevertheless be seen as the embryo of a political party that one day could threaten the Communist Party's monopoly over power. Twenty years later, exiled in New York, Wang Juntao told me he had expected to play a significant political role in China. His ambitions, however, would be carried away in the Tiananmen debacle.

In the spring of 1989, China was a real powder keg. While most Chinese were living better than in the days following the Cultural Revolution, in their eyes Deng's economic modernization was mainly synonymous with corruption, inequality, and uncertainty. On university campuses, students criticized the Communist Party and its leaders with total impunity. In the streets, the Chinese were no longer afraid to give free rein to their opinions. Even Communist leaders from the provinces called for more transparency and asked that friends and relatives of members of the Central Committee suspected of corruption be punished. The government was divided and the people knew it. In order to support reformers such as Zhao Ziyang, whom people sensed was wavering, the Chinese increased the pressure on their leaders. In such an unstable environment, Hu Yaobang's death on April 15 opened the floodgates of protest.

Deng Xiaoping was smoking when he was informed that Hu had just died of a heart attack. According to witnesses, he crushed his cigarette butt, crossed his hands pensively for a few seconds, then lit another cigarette. The sudden death of his old companion stunned Deng. The timing could not have been worse, two weeks before the May 4 celebrations and at a time when the government seemed more divided than ever. Probably out of a concern for unity, the Central Committee agreed to hold a grandiose funeral for Hu and shower him with unanimous praise. But the students quickly outmanoeuvred the party by using Hu's death as a pretext to demonstrate for reforms. They basically scuttled any plans the Chinese leadership had to use Hu's funeral to its advantage. From the day after the announcement of his death, more than ten thousand students showed up in Tiananmen Square to pay spontaneous homage to him. They placed sprays of flowers at the foot of the Monument to the People's Heroes and made speeches in the memory of the man they considered the father of the reforms now being threatened by the party's conservative wing. Art students painted a three-metre-high portrait of Hu. They paraded it around the square before standing it prominently against the Monument to the People's Heroes. In doing so, they imitated the students who had occupied Tiananmen Square in the days following Zhou Enlai's death in 1976. Their praise of Zhou had been an indirect way of criticizing Mao. Also, by demanding Hu Yaobang's name be rehabilitated, the students in 1989 were attacking the current patriarch's failure to act. "Yaobang is dead, but Xiaoping still lives,"[9] one poster read.

It soon became apparent that the students' intentions went far beyond a simple homage to Hu Yaobang. A few hundred of them, led by Wang Dan and Guo Haifeng, both from Beijing University, showed up in front of the entrance to the People's Palace and demanded a meeting with a senior government leader. They produced a list of seven demands, including restoring Hu Yaobang's views on democracy, publishing information on the income of state leaders and their family members, authorizing publication of privately run newspapers, raising intellectuals' pay, ending restrictions on holding demonstrations in Beijing, and conducting democratic elections to replace government officials who had made bad policy decisions. They also "demanded that the government-controlled media print and broadcast their demands and that the government respond to them publicly."[10] The way in which the students drew up the list of their demands reveals how improvised things were in these first days of demonstrations. When Wang Dan arrived at Tiananmen Square at the head of a few hundred Beijing University students, a student leader from another university, Zhang Boli, asked him what the goal of their demonstration was. "I do not know either," retorted Wang Dan. "It is you guys who initiated this." They then agreed to set up a list of demands.[11]

Their demands immediately hit a wall. No government representative came out to meet them. Frustrated, the students began singing "The Internationale" and moved toward the entrance of the Zhongnanhai complex, northwest of Tiananmen Square, where the offices of Deng Xiaoping, Zhao Ziyang, and other members of the Central Committee were located. Such audacity was very unusual. Since the time of the emperors, the gate was what separated the people from their leaders. It consisted of enormous red wooden doors flanked by two stone lions. The Chinese were strictly forbidden from entering. Yet here were students shoving police officers blocking their way, trying to force their way into the sanctuary of Communist leadership. "Li Peng, come out!" they chanted to the premier. Then: "Down with dictatorship, long live democracy!"

In the government quarters, the first cracks appeared in the strategy on how to deal with the students' unexpected action. Premier Li Peng, a hard-liner and already the main target of the demonstrators, recommended nipping the movement in the bud. Zhao Ziyang advocated tolerance. He said he was convinced the students' actions were inoffensive and that they were seeking to support the government's efforts of reform. Zhao ordered police offers guarding the Xinhua Gate to prevent students from passing but to remove the bayonets from their weapons to avoid any incident that could increase the tension.[12] These revelations about the divisions among the Chinese leaders during the Tiananmen Square crisis are found in *The Tiananmen Papers*.

The events occurring in Beijing and in other cities in China in late April 1989 were quite simply remarkable. Thanks to a mix of daring, idealism, and improvisation, in a few weeks the students managed to form a movement able to stand up to the Communist regime with the support of a large part of the population. They completely stole the sense of initiative from Chinese authorities, who were compelled to react to the events. When the government finally proposed a dialogue through officially recognized student organizations, the students refused and founded their own independent associations. The Beijing University Association was created in a night of euphoria, with no formal vote. Wang Dan convened hundreds of students to a democracy salon. Wang and the other student spokespersons knew they had to better structure their action and give themselves decision-making authority. They analyzed past student struggles and concluded these had failed because formal leadership was lacking. When he addressed the students, Wang Dan simply announced that "anyone who has the courage to stand up, give his name, his major, and what class he's in is automatically a member."[13] Seven students, including Wang, were elected to the steering committee. They adopted the list of demands that they had tried unsuccessfully to give the government and added a new one: the release of dissident Wei Jingsheng.

Elsewhere, creating a student association might seem commonplace, but in China it was an act of rebellion. To start with, it was illegal. The constitution forbade creating social groups outside those sanctioned by the party. But there was more. In rejecting the legitimacy of official associations, Wang Dan and the other student leaders challenged the very representativeness of the Communist Party. When, a few days later, they asked to negotiate directly with the government, they added insult to injury, as they claimed to speak with Chinese leaders as equals. To an outsider, this nuance may appear subtle, but the Chinese knew how important it was: the students had the audacity to raise themselves to the level of the emperor.

The students' deliberations had no secrets from the government, which had informers everywhere. The day after the founding of Beijing University's independent association, Communist leaders had a complete report of the event in hand. Authorities were also very well informed about what was going on in Tiananmen Square, where thousands of Chinese continued to flock in the days preceding Hu Yaobang's public funeral. An activity report was dispatched to the party every two hours. Plainclothes officers even questioned demonstrators to learn more about their motivation. Thus a middle-aged man who looked like a "civil servant" seemed to represent the opinion of the majority, one security officer reported. He said they were unhappy with the economic situation, didn't like the infighting within the government, and wanted more democracy and reform. Hu Yaobang was popular because he had been honest, open, and straightforward, "not like some of the corrupt leaders who are now on top."[14]

The elders of the Central Committee, who were among the most conservative members of the regime, showed signs of panic. The following telephone conversation, between Peng Zhen and Chen Xitong, was typical of the anxiety. "With Beijing in chaos like this we've got to guard against a 'second Cultural Revolution,'" said Peng to Chen. Both were convinced that the whole thing was fomented by foreign agents. "There must be some black hands behind these students, so we'd better get to the bottom of things."[15] The day of Hu Yaobang's funeral, even greater numbers of students showed up in Tiananmen Square. Wang Zhen, who, like other dignitaries, had to bypass the protestors to reach the ceremony, went to see Deng Xiaoping and implored him to have the police intervene to disperse the students. But Deng did not yet share the veterans' frustration. He told Wang the affair was not so simple and that it wasn't the time to talk about it.

During the first days of the student protests, the patriarch seemed ready to leave things up to his general secretary, Zhao Ziyang. To those who

recommended adopting a hard line, Zhao replied that the students were
motivated by a desire to improve the country and should not be seen as
enemies of the government. The day after Hu's funeral, Zhao Ziyang
nevertheless called a meeting of the politburo to find a way to contain the
student protests. First, Zhao told them, now that Hu Yaobang's memorial
service was over, they had to prevent the students from demonstrating and
get them to return to class. They had to avoid all violence, he specified,
which would provide a pretext for troublemakers. Then, he continued,
they had to punish those who engaged in acts of vandalism, but it was
important to do so in accordance with the law, not arbitrarily. Finally, said
Zhao Ziyang, they had to adopt a conciliatory approach to the students
and begin to dialogue with them. According to the minutes of the meeting,
Deng Xiaoping was in full agreement with Zhao's suggestions. "Good,"
he said when Zhao finished his presentation.[16] Confident of Deng's support
and his own position, Zhao informed politburo members that the following
day he would leave as planned for a state visit to North Korea. Cancelling
the visit would give the impression the government was weakening in the
face of the students' actions. Zhao asked his assistants to publish articles in
the official press emphasizing the positive aspect of the student demonstrations.
Then he designated Li Peng to replace him during his absence. It was an
error that would cost him dearly.

Far from subsiding, as Zhao Ziyang supposed, in the days following Hu
Yaobang's funeral, the student movement intensified, and each move by the
government only fanned the students' frustration. The students were at a
crossroads. All their requests for dialogue with the government had failed.
The last — where three students kneeled on the steps of the People's Palace,
imploring Li Peng to listen to them the way citizens used to do before the
emperor — touched a nerve with students and the population. Neither the
premier nor any other official deigned leave the palace to acknowledge their
presence and receive their demands. In times past, it was the mandarins'
duty to respectfully accept the people's petitions, even though they rarely

followed through on them. Many students were deeply humiliated by the symbolism of the incident. Wang Dan and the other student leaders knew they had to increase their pressure tactics, change strategies, or pack up. On April 26, no less than ten thousand of them gathered on a football field at Beijing University to decide the next step. They agreed without hesitation to the student leaders' proposal to boycott classes.

Learning the students had launched a general strike, Li Peng was furious. The act, he declared to his assistants, amounted to "a naked declaration of war against the Party."[17] The premier decided it was time for the leaders of each university to put an end to the nonsense. The authorities assembled the heads of seventy Beijing universities and ordered them to have the students listen to reason. They gave instructions to the teaching staff and campus party officials to mingle with students and convince them to abandon their strike and return to class. The tactic was a total fiasco; above all it revealed how cut off the Chinese government was from the students' reality. When university officials tried to convince them they were manipulated by a few radical elements, the students ridiculed them. The reality was that many professors supported the students' cause. Furthermore, the reports dispatched to Li Peng's office documented the administrations' total incapacity to influence the students. The results, they concluded, were "negligible." Worse, students took control of the universities' loudspeaker systems and used them to broadcast their demands even more widely. Even the physical layout of the universities put authorities at a disadvantage. After the Cultural Revolution, when the government decided to create several universities, it had concentrated the campuses to the northwest of the city, far from the seat of government, where it could easily control the students. The strategy worked for as long as the students were submissive to the party. But in the spring of 1989, this concentration of hundreds of thousands of students in one area strengthened their movement. The government simply lost control of the campuses.

Far from following Zhao Ziyang's directive to dialogue with the students, Li Peng decided to form a crisis unit to try to contain the protest movement.

Flanked by conservative elders of the government, he went to see Deng Xiaoping and told him about the escalation of demonstrations and the need for the government to get tough. The "spear" of the student protests is aimed personally at you, Li Peng told Deng Xiaoping, you and the other members of the generation of the "revolutionary proletariat." In the absence of Zhao Ziyang's moderating influence, the hard-liners seemed to have little difficulty convincing Deng Xiaoping he needed to act firmly to put an end to the protests. "I completely agree with the Standing Committee's decision," declared Deng. "This is no ordinary student movement," he added "but a well-planned plot whose real aim is to reject the Chinese Communist Party.... We've got to be explicit and clear in opposing this turmoil."[18] Armed with Deng's verdict, Li Peng suggested that his words be quoted in an editorial in the *People's Daily*.

The editorial would be a defining moment in the events of the spring of 1989. By describing the students' action as "turmoil" and accusing them of "conspiracy," the editorial used terms synonymous in the Chinese imagination with the anarchy of the Cultural Revolution. It was Deng, in fact, who personally insisted on using the term "turmoil."[19] But the editorial went further. It accused the student leaders of wanting to put an end to the reforms. If we show indulgence in the face of this turmoil, said the text written by the head of propaganda, we will have disorder. The reforms that the government, the population, and a majority of well-intentioned students want, the end of corruption, control of inflation, development of democracy, in short, a better life, will be impossible. The argument was both clever and inflammatory. The government, the editorial basically said, shared the population's grievances and wanted to accelerate China's democratization. But agitators in the student population were undermining these efforts.

Ironically, the April 26 editorial gave new momentum to the student movement that after a week was beginning to lose steam. After enduring repeated refusals from the Communist leadership to their requests for dialogue, Wang Dan and the other student leaders were indeed short of ideas about how to pursue their campaign. The editorial, however, galvanized the students into action. The following day, hundreds of thousands of them walked in the streets of Beijing. Not only did the police not intervene to prevent them from marching, but several of them openly said they sympathized with the students' demands. When workers, teachers, and even civil servants joined the march, it became obvious that the students' struggle had become the struggle of a large part of the population. Aware that the slightest incident could give credence to the editorial that accused them of being manipulated by a few troublemakers, the students showed iron discipline. They also tried to avoid antagonizing the Communist leadership. They marched with banners quoting Deng Xiaoping and Lenin on the issue of democracy and broke into a well-known patriotic song: "Without the Communist Party, There Would Be No New China." Some, aware of the presence of foreign television cameras, held up signs on which they had written "Vive la liberté!" in French or "Give me freedom or death" in English.

Li Peng was convinced the editorial would prompt students to give up their protest and return to class. He was wrong. Protests broke out in more than ten other cities. The heads of the universities in Beijing, who had been instructed to organize study sessions to spread the message of the April 26 editorial, reported that the exercise had failed. Even professors refused to attend. They told the government there was only one way to defuse the tension: begin a true dialogue with the students. When Li Peng convened the members of the politburo to take stock of the situation, the minister of public security reported a strong level of support for the students among officials and even among the military in several regions of the country. The premier said he was still convinced the agitation was the doing of a few people "calling the shots."[20] Nevertheless he consented to start discussions with students. But Li could not accept the government holding discussions solely with the protesters. He thus asked the State Council spokesperson, Yuan Mu, to convene the leaders of official student associations who supported the party and had not taken to the streets. A few of the representatives of what the government called illegal student associations, such as

Wang Dan, were also invited. Wang Dan refused the invitation. But others went, which created the first division among the student leaders.

It was a clever move. The students, in these conditions, were incapable of forming a united front. The exercise was like a one-way street. The official designated by Li Peng to talk with the students, Yuan Mu, was a former journalist and an excellent communicator. He made every effort to defend the government's integrity in front of the forty-five student representatives. He argued there were no serious problems of corruption. As proof, he said, the party leaders had cancelled their annual retreat to the beach resort of Beidaihe and prohibited the import of foreign luxury cars. He acknowledged some criticism, such as the student accusation that Zhao Ziyang played too much golf, the bourgeois sport par excellence. Li Peng congratulated Yuan Mu for his performance and ordered the meeting broadcast over state television. Li did not understand that China was facing a new political geography: it was no longer enough to deny reality for it to disappear and students would no longer accept the Communist Party's facade of democracy. Furthermore, the broadcast of the dialogue session, in which Yuan Mu made every effort to dodge even the most inoffensive questions of official student leaders, had the opposite effect. New demonstrations took place in several cities. In a press conference, Wang Dan described the exercise as a sham.

When he returned from North Korea the next day, Zhao Ziyang still believed he could gain control of the situation. He convened a meeting of a politburo subcommittee, intending to soften the government's tone to the students. The minutes of the meeting reveal the unbridgeable gap separating Zhao from his premier, Li Peng. After an initial first discussion in which obvious concern could be felt among the other members of the politburo, Zhao gave a detailed presentation, practically endorsing the students' position. No Communist leader had ever gone so far in his criticism of the system. One month later, Zhao Ziyang's words served as evidence when he was expelled from the party.

"Times have changed," said Zhao Ziyang, "and so have people's ideological views. Democracy is a worldwide trend, and there is an international counter-current against communism and socialism that flies under the banners of democracy and human rights. If the party doesn't hold up the banner of democracy in our country, someone else will, and we will lose out."[21] In his memoirs, Zhao Ziyang wrote that he still hoped at that time to use the student protests to relaunch his political reforms. But he remained cautious before the committee. He was careful to reaffirm the party's supremacy. "We must, of course," he said, "insist on Communist Party leadership and not play around with any Western multiparty systems." But the party, he added, must change its way of governing and increase transparency. All the party leaders, he said, had to learn to work and live in a system founded on democracy and law. "In sum, we must make the people feel that under the leadership of the Communist Party and the socialist system they can truly and fully enjoy democracy and freedom."[22] As a token of the government's good faith, Zhao believed the April 26 editorial had to be corrected immediately. But he only received the support of one member of the politburo, a reformer like himself, Hu Qili. The others sided with Li Peng, who was firmly opposed to retracting the editorial. What the students were doing, he said, was illegal. The only way to resolve the crisis, he said, was to re-establish stability. Then they could speak of dialogue and reform.

On May 3, at a speech commemorating the anniversary of the Movement of May 4, 1919, Zhao Ziyang asserted publicly what he stated to the politburo. The government had to show the students understanding and must exercise restraint. The students were not rejecting the system, he said, only the gaps in it. Their demands had to be dealt with in a context of "democracy and legality." Zhao, whose speech had been written by Bao Tong, used the same arguments before the Asian Development Bank the next day. It had no effect upon the students. More than fifty thousand of them marched on Tiananmen Square to commemorate the anniversary of May 4, breaking out into patriotic songs from the 1930s. "Tomorrow," they sang, "we will rise in a powerful wave to defend our country." It was as if the entire country had heard their call. Two days later, no less than a million and a half students in eighty cities took to the streets to support the protests in Beijing. It was not only students that converged on Tiananmen Square: members of labour organizations and five hundred journalists from the official press showed up, demanding the right to speak the truth, to no longer be muzzled by censors.

While the regime did not budge, it was concerned. "If the workers rise up," said one member of the politburo, "we are really in a mess." Wrongly believing the government's silence meant it was ready to strike hard and arrest them, student leaders decided to raise the stakes. "We needed more radical methods to force the government to comply with our demands," Wang Dan remembers. "Since the demonstrations no longer had any effect, we agreed to start a hunger strike." The following day, after one last symbolic dinner, a thousand students, including Wang Dan and the woman who would become the radical voice of the movement, Chai Ling, began their fast. Their crusade for reform, which until then had seemed rational and tactical, now became emotional, almost desperate. Addressing more than a thousand people at Tiananmen Square, Chai Ling, voice choked with emotion, declared the authorities were forcing students to risk their lives. "We want to see if the Chinese have a conscience," she proclaimed, "and if there is still hope for China. We are ready to face death to ensure a new life." Zhao Ziyang immediately recognized this was a dangerous escalation. He wanted at all costs to avoid the students becoming martyrs. Certain demonstrators even used their own blood to write slogans on banners. Only one of them had to die for the situation to degenerate completely. Zhao immediately sent Bao Tong to try to dissuade the students from proceeding with their hunger strike. But they refused to speak to him, calling him "neo-authoritarian." They had failed to recognize the few allies they had within the party leadership or, at this point, didn't care.

With the hunger strike, the student movement became more radical. Wang Dan, who was perceived as a voice of reason, became increasingly overshadowed by Chai Ling, who would soon become known as the Joan of Arc of the movement. The moderates in both camps were being marginalized. Wang Juntao and other moderate intellectuals, who hoped to play the role of midwives of reform, were aware the window of compromise was closing rapidly. General Secretary Zhao Ziyang nevertheless made a new attempt at conciliation with the students. He appointed Yan Mingfu, one of his reformer allies, to negotiate a pact with the students that would allow Tiananmen Square to be freed before Mikhail Gorbachev's expected visit to Beijing on May 15. Yan asked Wang Juntao and Chen Zeming to identify the student leaders whom he was most likely to reason with. For Wang Juntao, this was perhaps the last chance to avoid the worst. He had feared the army would intervene from the first days of the occupation of Tiananmen Square, as it had done in 1976 when he, with others, ended up in prison for daring to commemorate the death of Zhou Enlai. He knew that Deng Xiaoping's patience would not last forever. With his colleague Chen Zeming, Wang had already formed a coordination group that met with student leaders regularly to try to influence their strategy. "I had two objectives in mind," Wang told me twenty years later. "On one hand, the student leadership had to be structured as it was starting to divide up into factions. On the other, I needed to coordinate the disparate demands arising from all sides so as to have just one negotiating position with the government." For three days, Wang and Chen went back and forth between Yan, Zhao Ziyang's emissary, and the student leaders, negotiating the meeting place, the number of participants, as well as the agenda of the negotiations. They briefed the students on the various factions in the government, told them the authorities were desperate for a way out of the crisis, and recommended they try to avoid any provocation that would undermine the reformers' position and prove the hard-liners right.

Despite all these precautions, the meeting failed. The students demanded the session be broadcast live on state television. Yan Mingfu told them this was impossible, but that their discussions would be broadcast on the radio. One of the spokespersons of the moderate faction, Shen Tong, who had led the march against the editorial in the *People's Daily* with Wang Dan, then set out the students' demands. He didn't have time to finish his account before one of the representatives of the hunger strikers activated a tape recorder on which he had recorded new demands. After a brief consultation, the students agreed to focus on the first demand: retraction of the April 26 editorial. The session, however, ended there. At the same time, learning that the session was not broadcast on television or radio, a group of students began protesting at the doors to the building. In view of the agitation, the members of the student delegation decided to withdraw from the negotiations. They went to Tiananmen Square to inform the hunger strikers that negotiations had failed. "The atmosphere was so emotional it was impossible for us to continue," remembers Wang Dan. Yan Mingfu made a report of his discussions to Zhao Ziyang. He was pessimistic. The students, he said, were not in agreement among themselves. They didn't even sit together. "I don't know if any of them really represents the hunger strikers or can exert the slightest of influence on them." The following day, Yan again tried to convince students of the government's good faith. He told them they represented the future, that they were essential to the reform movement, and swore that the issue of the offensive editorial would be settled. "If you don't believe me, you can take me hostage,"[23] he added as a last resort.

A group of twelve intellectuals, writers, and academics also attempted a rapprochement between the government and the students. Dai Qing, their spokesperson, addressed the demonstrators in Tiananmen Square and asked them to compromise. He offered to take their demands to Yan Mingfu, the government's representative. Yan Mingfu told the intellectuals that the students, in exchange, should agree to free Tiananmen Square at least temporarily. "What do they want exactly?" he asked. Dai Qing replied that the students were ready to leave on three conditions: the government leaders must personally declare that the student movement was patriotic and democratic, that the new student associations were legal, and that there would be no reprisals against the demonstrations. "That's absolutely unworkable," replied Yan Mingfu.[24] The students, he said, were getting greedier. If they stopped adding conditions, perhaps Zhao Ziyang and Li Peng would consider meeting with them. Dai Qing returned to Tiananmen

Square to make a last appeal to the students. "You have proved that all of China is demanding democracy. But democratization takes time," he told them. He asked them to free the square. He was booed and returned empty-handed. "We intellectuals were caught between a totally irrational government and totally irrational students. What could we do?"[25] he said. The most radical wing of the student movement from then on took control of the events. The next day, Mikhail Gorbachev arrived in Beijing accompanied by a significant contingent of foreign journalists. Tiananmen would now become an event of international significance.

★ ★ ★

For Deng Xiaoping and the Chinese leaders, the humiliation was complete. The ceremony welcoming Mikhail Gorbachev planned for Tiananmen Square had to be cancelled. Due to the presence of protesters, the Soviet leader was forced to use a back entrance to the Great Hall of the People for his meeting with Deng Xiaoping. Invigorated by Gorbachev's arrival, the demonstrators came to Tiananmen Square in greater numbers. There were even representatives from the fashion industry and civil servants in charge of dealing with natural disasters. Soldiers relinquished their uniforms and dressed in civilian clothes to take part in the demonstrations. Police officers were seen playing cards on the steps of the Great Hall, applauding the speeches. An even more worrisome sign for the government: thousands of students arrived by train from other cities in China to join the movement. Dan Rather, CBS's star correspondent, reported that Tiananmen Square now belonged to the people. "More than a million Chinese are demanding democracy and freedom and proclaiming a new revolution," he announced to America.

In his meeting with Gorbachev, Zhao Ziyang tried to reassure the Soviet leader. The reforms, he said, could satisfy students expressing doubts about socialism. In any case, he added, even if Deng Xiaoping no longer had an official function in the government, he still resolved important issues. This indiscretion regarding Deng's role would cost him dearly. It was the beginning of the end for Zhao, whose influence scattered like sand in the wind. He called a meeting of the politburo subcommittee to announce he would write a letter to the students guaranteeing them immunity if they stopped their demonstrations. But Zhao no longer had the politburo's support. In the face of the impasse, he and Li Peng decided to leave the matter up to Deng. On May 17, they showed up at Deng's residence with other members of the subcommittee. Once there, Li Peng and his allies launched an all-out attack against Zhao. Li accused the general secretary of being responsible for the escalation of the protest movement. Vice-Prime Minister Yao Yilin jumped in, saying that Zhao had revealed divisions in the party in his speech before the Asian Development Bank. Then he accused him of wanting to blame Deng for the crisis by telling Gorbachev that the patriarch still played a determining role in leadership decisions. Zhao tried his best to defend himself. But Deng dealt him a lethal blow. The situation really began to deteriorate, he said, from the moment Zhao became conciliatory in his speeches. Opening the door to multiple-party elections like in the West, he continued, would lead to the kind of civil war China had experienced during the Cultural Revolution. If things continue, he warned, we are likely to be placed under arrest. Then he uttered his final verdict: they had to call in the army and declare martial law! Zhao Ziyang told Deng he could not accept this decision. "The minority yields to the majority!" Deng reminded him. "I will submit to party discipline,"[26] replied Zhao. But as soon as he returned home, he summoned Bao Tong and asked him to write his letter of resignation. Zhao, however, did not submit it immediately. The following day, during a special meeting of the politburo subcommittee, he tried one last time to convince Li Peng and the others not to impose martial law. "It could cost us what remains of our legitimacy," he declared. But Li Peng was uncompromising. Zhao Ziyang gave up. His opinions on the student movement, he told them, differed from those of Deng Xiaoping and the majority of the committee. In those conditions, he continued, how could he remain general secretary? The following evening, Zhao made his final public appearance. He went to Tiananmen Square and, with tears in his eyes, told the students: "We have come but too late."[27] The hard-liners now had free rein.

★ ★ ★

Meanwhile, the hunger strike was transforming the dynamic of the student movement. More than three thousand people had now joined it. On their fourth day of fasting, dozens of students began to lose consciousness. There were not enough ambulances to shuttle back and forth between Tiananmen Square and the hospitals. But as soon as they were revived, many of them returned to fast. The Chinese, horrified by the sight of their youth wasting away while the government turned a deaf ear to their demands, converged on Tiananmen Square to show their support. The minister of security estimated there were one million, two hundred thousand of them. Facing what was possibly the greatest popular demonstration in the history of China, on the morning of May 18, Li Peng, the regime's new strongman, finally agreed to meet the student leaders. The meeting the students had been demanding was set for eleven o'clock at the Great Hall of the People, the Chinese parliament. Wang Dan and Wu'er Kaixi, two student leaders who had started the movement, were chosen to speak with Li Peng. The scene was surreal. Li Peng, flanked by his assistants, was seated in a big lace-covered armchair. Across from him, in a semicircle, were the student leaders. Wu'er Kaixi, who was taking part in the hunger strike, arrived from the hospital in pyjamas.

The meeting would mark the final break between the students and the government. From the start, Li Peng refused to discuss the students' demands. They had to focus on one subject, he said: to find a way to put an end to the hunger strike. But he was immediately interrupted by Wu'er Kaixi. "We're not here because you invited us," he said to the premier, "but because of the hundreds and thousands of students in the square who invited you to talk to us. We must decide the number of topics, not you."[28] Wang Dan carried on by saying that to put an end to the hunger strike, the government had to give in to the students' demands. The government, he told Li Peng, who had remained impassive ever since the students took control of the meeting, had to realize that the student movement was patriotic and needed to begin a real dialogue. As leader of the movement's moderate faction,

Wang Dan still hoped the government would agree to discuss things, which would allow them to end the occupation of Tiananmen Square and launch the student movement on a new basis in the fall. But it was already too late. The hunger strikers sent a written message to their representatives asking them to put an end to the meeting with Li Peng. The conclusion of the meeting was worthy of a movie. Li Peng held out a hand to one of the students, who refused to shake it, a humiliating and unforgivable affront to the Communist leader. Then Wu'er Kaixi, weakened by his fast, fainted. Li Peng, visibly appalled by the students' treatment of him, left the Great Hall. All that remained was for him to sign the decree imposing martial law.

On the morning of May 20, twenty-two divisions of the People's Army converged on the strategic areas of Beijing to enforce martial law. Then something occurred that no one, not even the government, had predicted. Ordinary Chinese came out of their homes and blocked the path of the military. Workers set up makeshift barricades in the street; grandmothers shouted abuse at soldiers, telling them they should be ashamed of attacking the people like this; girls gave bouquets of flowers to the recruits. In many neighbourhoods, the military put down their rifles, sat on their tanks, and bantered with people. It became obvious that the military leadership itself was divided on the issue of martial law. Eight generals and two marshals refused to obey orders. They deemed martial law too drastic a measure. After a great deal of pressure, they nevertheless agreed to rally, without great enthusiasm.[29] But not General Xu Qinxian, commander of the Thirty-Eighth Army. He was dismissed from his duties and sent to hospital. Four days after the decree of martial law, however, things were still at an impasse; Beijingers continued to block the way of the military. The government, fearing the military would be contaminated by too much contact with the people, ordered soldiers to retreat to the city limits, and took advantage of this to replace many soldiers with detachments from faraway provinces, deemed to be more loyal. This all-important decision would ensure the success of the June 4 operation.

Many Chinese wrongly believed the government would not dare order the military to fire on the people. Wang Juntao saw the lull as an opportunity to attempt a political show of force. The idea, which he discussed with Bao Tong, other intellectuals, and student leaders, was to try to convince the People's Congress, the Chinese parliament, to overturn martial law. Considering the tension reigning in the capital and the enormous opposition to martial law throughout the country, they believed the delegates could be brought to defy Li Peng and the elders. Wan Li, president of the People's Congress and member of the politburo, was travelling in Canada when he came out publicly against martial law. If he agreed to submit the question of martial law to a vote in congress, anything could happen.

On the morning of May 27, Wang Juntao, Chen Zeming, and other intellectuals assembled the leaders of the student movement in a room in the Academy of Sciences. Wang Dan, with others, advocated ending the occupation of Tiananmen Square. The movement, he believed, had accomplished all it could hope to; they needed to use the summer to regroup and prepare a new political offensive in the fall. The independent student association he led had already announced its intention to withdraw from Tiananmen following a final monster protest on May 29. Wang read the text of a proposal that quite obviously had been written with the help of Wang Juntao. If the People's Congress reversed the decision to impose martial law at its meeting on June 20, the students would leave Tiananmen Square. Chai Ling, the leader of the movement's most radical wing, surprised many by agreeing with the proposal. She said she was tired, confused, and did not believe the students could hold their siege much longer. Wang Juntao and Wang Dan left the meeting believing they had found a way out that would avoid military intervention. Back at Tiananmen Square, however, Chai Ling reversed her stand. She could not bring herself to announce to the demonstrators that the fight was over. Many of them were students who had come from the provinces and who wanted to have it out with the government. The student consensus only lasted for a morning. It was to be Wang Dan's swan song. Two days later, the thousands of students who still occupied Tiananmen Square decided to dismiss him from his duties. Resigned, Wang Dan headed back to Beijing University. "How could I control anything?" he told me twenty years later in London. "I was so young and the student movement had become an uncontrollable mass."

In any case, the hope of overthrowing martial law through the People's Congress was doomed to fail. Learning of the project, Deng Xiaoping called back Wan Li, the president of the People's Congress, from his trip in North America. The government kept him in Shanghai to prevent his from trying to organize a vote on martial law. He was forbidden to return to Beijing until he publicly supported it, which he did eventually. In late May it became clear that Deng Xiaoping and the elders had resolved to regain control of operations. From then on, the important decisions were made at Deng's residence and not at the politburo meetings. The patriarch was especially appalled at the government and the army's inability to have martial law respected. He held Zhao personally responsible for this state of things. On May 21, Zhao was dismissed. He had never formally handed in his resignation. When he showed up at the office the next day, he found it empty.

According to the minutes of discussions that appear in *The Tiananmen Papers*, Deng Xiaoping seemed sincerely saddened to have to dismiss his heir apparent. He realized that the third generation of leaders represented by Zhao did not have the firmness required to quell the student revolt. If the party made an error, said Deng, it was in not insisting sufficiently on educating the population. China's modernization could not occur without the exclusive leadership of the Communist Party, said Deng, adding it was essential to put an end to the student revolt. A new team had to be appointed to defend the four modernizations and ensure the Communist Party's supremacy. He suggested Zhao be replaced as general secretary by Jiang Zemin, the strongman of the party in Shanghai, an official who had business sense and had shown determination in the face of the student demonstrations.

The decision to have the army intervene to free Tiananmen Square was made on the morning of June 2. Deng presented his analysis of the situation in detail. The causes of the turmoil, he said, did not stem from conditions inside China but from a propaganda offensive from the West that sought to usurp the Chinese government's authority. The United States in particular, said Deng, encouraged and helped the "so-called democrats" in China who "are the scum of the Chinese nation."[30] This distrust of the American role was surely confirmed by the appearance of a gigantic Styrofoam effigy of the Statue of Liberty in Tiananmen Square that students called the Goddess of Democracy. Stability, Deng concluded, must take precedence over everything else. The government could not modernize China if it had to deal constantly with chaos. "That's why," said Deng, "we have to insist on clearing the square." Yet first, he said, they had to try to persuade the students to leave the square. "But if they refuse to leave," he warned, "they will be responsible for the consequences."[31]

In the night of June 3 to 4, 1989, the military advanced on Tiananmen Square. Hundreds, perhaps thousands, of Chinese died trying to block their way. After swearing to hold out until death, the students who remained, including Chai Ling, agreed to safe conduct and vacated Tiananmen Square without resistance. Wang Juntao, alerted by his driver, left to seek the student leaders he wanted to smuggle out of Beijing. It took him three days to gather them together. Wang Dan was among them. He was completely lost and didn't know what to do, he told me. Wang Juntao took them by train to Harbin, where he hoped they could more easily escape the police roundup. From Harbin they took a plane to Shanghai, where they decided to separate. Wang Juntao was arrested a few weeks later in the south of China trying to buy a train ticket. As for Wang Dan, he was not cut out to be a fugitive. Fearing he would compromise the people putting him up in Shanghai, he decided to return to Beijing and not stay in hiding. The police arrested him shortly after he arrived. A few weeks earlier, Wang Dan, with others, had represented China's democratic future. Now he would begin the existence of a political prisoner. His life would be one of dissidence and exile. The Chinese government could not bring itself to accept Wang Dan and the millions of other Chinese who called for change and the country's transformation. In the image of the young student leader, the Chinese democratic movement now entered a period of hibernation.

With the Tiananmen Square massacre, the political reform movement that had inspired so many Chinese in the 1980s was basically wiped out. Could it have been otherwise? Did the students force the government's hand, impatient at the slowness of the reforms? Had they inadvertently pulled the rug from under the feet of the reformers in the government? When we examine reports of the Chinese leaders' discussions, it becomes quite clear that the patriarch Deng Xiaoping could not reconcile himself with the idea of a Western-style democracy. That was too much to ask from the old revolutionary who had devoted his life to building the Communist Party. The purge that would follow the Tiananmen crisis would wipe out the reformist wing within the party leadership and establish a hard line on political reform that persists today. In the immediate aftermath of Tiananmen, it would also threaten the very thing Deng meant to protect by cracking down on the student movement: the economic modernization of China.

7
Deng Xiaoping's Victory

Shenzhen, January 1992

Aware that his modernization program was in jeopardy, Deng Xiaoping began a highly symbolic visit to the new free economic zone of Shenzhen in the south of the country. Shenzhen is located right across from Hong Kong and is one of the manufacturing centres for companies relying on Chinese labour to produce goods for the world market. Deng had made it the showcase for foreign investment in China. This was not an easy undertaking for him; he was eighty-seven years old and suffering from Parkinson's disease. His daughter, who went with him, helped him get around. Despite his failing health, Deng was convinced he had to do something to prevent the conservatives in the politburo from backtracking on his economic model.

The local press reported that when Deng exited the train he seemed in good health, bright-eyed and wearing a "Western-style" grey jacket and black pants. Nothing was left to chance. Deng visited a factory that produced laser discs for Philips, the Dutch multinational. Then, from a revolving restaurant on the fifty-third floor of a commercial building overlooking what had been only a village fifteen years earlier, the patriarch invited the Chinese to redouble their efforts to make their economic modernization a success. In a scarcely veiled criticism of his opponents, he declared they had to put an end to "hollow speeches" and set about creating "useful things." He said they needed to be inspired by the "fruits of civilization," including those of "advanced capitalist societies." China, he continued, must act boldly and not like a "woman with bound feet," an expression Mao had been fond of to criticize people whose revolutionary fervour he doubted. China, said Deng, should be inspired by the model of what he called the "four little dragons" — Hong Kong, Singapore, South Korea, and Taiwan — and even surpass them. To people who claimed that was drifting toward capitalism, he retorted that, on the contrary, it was creating "socialism with Chinese characteristics."

eng Xiaoping's tour of the south of the country in 1992 is considered the turning point that allowed the patriarch to save his modernization program and launch China on the path of the industrial miracle that made it one of today's great economic powers. At the time, however, Deng's tour looked as if it would fail. Premier Li Peng and the other conservative elements in the Chinese leadership ordered the national press to ignore Deng's trip. Most Chinese didn't even know about it.

Deng was paying the price for the realignment of political forces he himself set in motion following the Tiananmen Square crisis. Minutes of meetings between Chinese leaders in the summer of 1989 reveal that Deng Xiaoping was very aware of the consequences of crushing the forces of reform in the party and the population. In a speech to the new team of leaders in mid-June 1989, less than two weeks after quelling the Tiananmen Square protests, Deng spoke of the need not only to pursue but also to accelerate economic reforms. The rest of the world was afraid China was closing in on itself, he said. They needed to demonstrate the opposite. That is why Deng did not want Zhao Ziyang to be tried publicly or for too many party officials sympathetic to the students to be dismissed. He wanted to put it all behind him quickly. A long settling of scores, such as during the Cultural Revolution, could sink his economic reforms. To renew people's confidence in the government, he proposed to lay charges of corruption against one or two dozen party leaders, public trials that would show that the government and the party were serious about reform. The success of his program depended upon it. "We've got to get our party in order," said Deng. "Our long-range plans may fail if we don't get rid of corruption, especially at the higher levels in the party."[1]

Deng announced at the same time his intention to withdraw from active politics. He wanted to give complete freedom to the third generation of leaders, led by Jiang Zemin, the former mayor of Shanghai who had stood up to the protestors and whom he designated as his successor. Deng warned the politburo he didn't even want an honorary position. He had seen how concentration of power in Mao's hands had led to excesses and how disastrous his cult of personality had been for China. He believed the Chinese had to put an end to these unhealthy tendencies. "If I have ideas that can be useful, I will definitely share them with the new leaders," he said.

With Deng withdrawing from power, no one in the Communist leadership remained who could actively promote economic modernization. For Premier Li Peng, in particular, the priority was to ensure the stability of the regime. In his eyes, the pace of economic reforms begun by Zhao Ziyang was largely responsible for the troubles in the spring of 1989. Li pushed through a law prohibiting demonstrations that questioned Communist Party's leadership.[2] He also launched a vast rectification campaign to ensure no radical elements remained in the party ranks. Even the military wasn't spared. In the winter of 1990, fearing the kind of rebellion that put an end to Nicolae Ceauşescu in Romania, Chinese leaders ordered an inquiry into the behaviour of several thousand officers in the People's Army. Many among them whose loyalty was deemed suspect were court-martialled and expelled from the ranks. Simultaneously, the government launched an indoctrination campaign in the ranks of the military to fight bourgeois liberalization and what it called the "peaceful evolution," a euphemism designating Western-style capitalist democracy. In order to show the Chinese that the leadership itself was ready to admit its errors and change its ways, the politburo announced that "children of [party] officials were banned from business, and top figures were to forego personal cars and foreign food."[3]

What Li Peng and the other conservatives in the politburo wanted was to turn back the clock on Deng's modernization. They proposed not only to slow down or put the brakes on economic liberalization but also to reject its core principles. The conservatives proposed ousting capitalist companies from the free economic zones that were the port of entry for foreign capital into China. They intended to hand back the monopoly of the large industrial sectors to state-owned enterprises. Some even went as far as to demand the recollectivization of agriculture. This ideological reversal reveals the conservatives' innate distrust of the market but also the life experiences that shaped Communist hard-liners such as Li Peng.

Li Peng was a pure product of the school of planned economy. After his parents were killed by Nationalist forces, Li Peng, then a child, was adopted by Zhou Enlai and his wife. He was sent to the USSR to complete his studies at the Moscow Energy Institute. He returned convinced that China's economic future lay in huge industrial projects. Li Peng is considered the father of the grandiose, controversial Three Gorges Dam project. With Zhao Ziyang's dismissal, the premier had a free hand in slowing down the economic modernization and in giving the state a greater role in the economy. In a direct affront to Deng, Li Peng declared that "reform and openness," the cornerstone of the patriarch's achievement, should no longer guide China's economic development. Wang Zhen, one of the elders, complained that the reforms favoured capitalism and foreign religions and undercut the Communist Party's ability to attract young people. He was right. Deng, aware he could no longer lean on reformers to keep conservatives in check, complained in an interview that no one paid attention to him anymore.

Two years after Tiananmen Square, Deng Xiaoping's very legacy seemed in danger. The pragmatism he managed to introduce into the Chinese economy was challenged by the new leadership's ideological rigidity. Abroad, the image of the new, more open China that he had worked so hard to build was in ruins, wiped out by the image of the tanks crushing the democratic momentum of Tiananmen Square. By repressing the student movement and appointing a new, firmer team, Deng wanted to re-establish political stability to ensure the survival of his economic reforms. But it was looking increasingly like a pyrrhic victory, for his modernization program could well be the price of this stability.

One of the great unknowns of this period was Jiang Zemin, the new general secretary. In many respects, he was like a work of abstract art: open to interpretation. Like many officials of his generation, Jiang was trained in the USSR, where he had even worked in a Moscow auto plant. Still, he was quite eclectic, a polyglot who could speak a half-dozen languages, including English, Russian, Romanian, and Japanese. He liked Chinese poetry and the music of Elvis Presley. Politically, he was said to be cautious rather than dogmatic. His round face, framed by large glasses, seemed permanently frozen in an enigmatic half-smile. He appeared as inscrutable as a sphinx. As a former mayor of Shanghai, a city with a long tradition of trade, one could have thought that Jiang was pragmatic. Shortly after his appointment, however, Jiang seemed to rally to the conservative consensus in the politburo.

Despite the conservatives' offensive, Deng remained very popular with the people — much more so than Jiang Zemin, who was not very well known, or Li Peng, who was known as the " Butcher of Tiananmen Square." The Chinese were grateful to Deng for bringing China out of the darkness of the Mao years and for greatly improving their standard of living. This wasn't the first time Deng was on the ropes politically. He had survived two purges under Mao before making a comeback, the last time following the Cultural Revolution, where he had been banished to the countryside. Deng called on the Chinese to fight those who wanted to scuttle his reforms.

The journey he began in January 1992 was his last and, possibly, the most important of his life. Deng left Wuhan in a private train bound for Shenzhen and Zhuhai, two free economic zones that symbolized China's openness to the world. Then he continued on to Shanghai, China's great economic metropolis. Historically, the Chinese emperors left the Forbidden City to take long journeys when they felt the need to renew the people's support. Deng followed this tradition. Beyond his calls for modernization, however, it was his famous saying that "to get rich is glorious" that struck people's imagination. It was as if Deng had lifted a taboo that dated from the revolution. He told the Chinese they could aspire to becoming rich and be good socialists at the same time.

It took several weeks for the report of his speeches to appear in the national press, but the effect was immediate. Money began to flow into the economic zones. After more than two years of uncertainty and hesitation, Deng refocused on modernization and openness. His initiative led to a realignment of political forces in the Chinese leadership. The reformers regained strength, whereas the conservatives were forced to back down.

Jiang Zemin, who leaned more to the side of the conservatives, understood the popular sentiment and stood behind Deng. The patriarch had an authority that Jiang did not, and Jiang realized this.

Deng's victory put an end to the tug-of-war that had lasted for more than ten years between the tenants of socialist dogmatism and people who like himself favoured pragmatism of the market. The two schools of thought, at first glance incompatible, were soon reconciled through a clever compromise: "socialism with Chinese characteristics." Deng's doctrine also contained a political component. The first condition for China's economic success was political stability. However, this was an ultimatum rather than a pact with the people or a social contract. The government told the Chinese it would devote its energy to modernizing China and guarantee them improved living conditions providing they did not get involved in politics. The trials of the main leaders of the Tiananmen Square movement and the heavy prison sentences they received were tangible proof that the government intended to tolerate no dissidence.

In the winter of 1992, when Deng began his southern tour, Wang Dan had been wilting for two and a half years in a cell at Qincheng, the famous prison for political prisoners. The first thing he did upon arriving in his cell was to measure it. It was seven steps long. He slept on a wooden board on the ground. There was a toilet with no cover in a corner. When he turned himself into authorities on July 2, 1989, after being on the run for less than a month, he was the most wanted man in China, the first on a list of twenty-one people whose photo was put up in train stations and public places.

Other student leaders were luckier. Chai Ling, the passionate activist of Tiananmen Square, managed to reach Hong Kong hidden in a wooden box in the hold of a boat. Li Lu, the student from Tianjin who joined the movement later and was one of its most radical leaders, also managed to flee China. Today they both have become rich entrepreneurs in the United States. Many of the most wanted fugitives received significant support from the people; some were hidden and fed for close to a year before they could make their escape. Five hundred of them reached Hong Kong thanks to a network of supporters who used smugglers. The fugitive received a coded message to go to a precise spot on China's south coast. He was picked up there, at night, by a small boat. With a bit of luck, its captain managed to escape the Chinese coast guard and numerous pirates who patrolled the stretch of sea separating the mainland from Hong Kong.

The authorities, however, managed to lay their hands on the two intellectuals they accused of being the "black hands" behind the movement, Wang Juntao and Chen Zeming. Both were subjected to a closed-door trial whose conclusion was known in advance. Each was sentenced to thirteen years in prison for attempting to usurp the powers of state, which amounts to treason. Bao Tong, the right hand of former general secretary Zhao Ziyang, who led the political reform group, completed the quartet of imprisoned star dissidents. He was found guilty of disclosing state secrets. He was criticized mainly for his meetings with American financier and philanthropist George Soros, whose foundation funded reform and democratization projects. The indictment, however, did not just stem from his meetings with Soros or his ideas of reform. "He wears gaudy jackets and blue jeans... what kind of a party official is that?"[4] one of the elders said when the Central Committee discussed Bao Tong's case.

Starting from when they were tried and imprisoned, a remarkable change occurred among the leaders of the Tiananmen Square movement. An American sociologist even spoke of a change of identity. At the very least it was a change in the role they saw for themselves in this Chinese society that had been politically lobotomized and that, as one historian said, from then on was only entitled to do business. Wang Dan, Wang Juntao, and Chen Zeming went from being the leaders of a reform movement to being martyrs for the cause of democracy. Bao Tong, older, more philosophical, did not seem surprised by the way his life was turning out; it was as if in a way he expected it. Not only did the young leaders of the movement have to find meaning in the long years they would spend in prison, many Chinese as well as a large part of the international community considered them to be peace offerings of the Tiananmen Square movement. What happened to them was not exceptional but in keeping with the fate historically reserved for partisans of democracy in China. From the Hundred Days' Reform to the Hundred Flowers Campaign, from the Democracy Wall to the Tiananmen Square massacre, the scenario for the democrats was the same. Even before he found himself at the forefront of the protest movement, Wang Dan was well aware he risked going to prison for his activities. He knew history. He even asked Ren Wanding, a veteran of the Democracy Wall of 1978 who had done time in prison, how to deal with life and the difficult prison conditions. Ren advised him to continue to speak out loud, even when alone in his cell, so his vocal cords and his ability to reason would not atrophy.

"I saw prison as a necessary stage in my commitment to the pro-democratic movement, like a compulsory course every dissident has to take to understand China's political reality," Wang Dan confided to me. "As I had chosen this path, I had to be ready for all the obstacles that would be in my way. That's what allowed me to remain optimistic." To stay in shape, Wang Dan forced himself to walk around his cell five hundred times a day. And he hummed "The Internationale," the great Communist hymn, while taking his exercise.

While the Chinese government intended to relegate the imprisoned dissidents to oblivion, it was powerless to change the symbol they were becoming abroad. Following their sentencing, in January 1991 the *New York Times* compared Wang Juntao and Chen Zeming to Czechoslovakian dissident Vaclav Havel and to Soviet dissident Anatoly Sharansky. Nor should we forget Wei Jingsheng, wrote the *Times* in an editorial, who had been rotting in prison in inhumane conditions for eleven years. The Chinese government was not completely insensitive to criticism from the international community. Wang Dan, Wang Juntao, and Wei Jingsheng were about to become bargaining chips in China's attempt to remake its image following the Tiananmen Square crisis.

Wang Dan was the first to be freed before the end of his sentence, in 1993, shortly before the visit of the International Olympic Committee (IOC) to Beijing. Five months remained in his four-year prison sentence.

Chinese authorities said he had shown he was rehabilitated, in particular by the work he'd done in prison. His release came very close to the IOC's decision on Beijing's Olympic bid. Even though he declared he intended to go into business upon leaving prison, Wang Dan started up his political activities again. He had invested too much in the cause to abandon it. He published articles on democracy and human rights in foreign magazines, maintained extensive correspondence with other dissidents, and started a support group for victims of Tiananmen Square. In 1995 he was arrested again, accused of wanting to overthrow the government, and sentenced to eleven years in prison.

Wei Jingsheng, the veteran of the Democracy Wall, was also freed suddenly before the end of his sentence, in the fall of 1993, in what would be interpreted as a sign of openness by the Chinese government only a few days before the IOC decided on Beijing's bid for the 2000 Summer Games. China was not selected for the Games, and Wei Jingsheng publicly denounced being used as a bargaining chip. Like Wang Dan, he started up his political activities again and soon found himself back in prison.

With Bill Clinton's arrival in the White House in 1992, imprisoned Chinese dissidents found themselves at the forefront of relations between the United States and China. At no moment in history, either before or after, has an American president invested so much political capital in his efforts to free the people he considered to be the political prisoners of Tiananmen Square. Close to twenty years later, in the spring of 2009, when Hillary Clinton, secretary of state and wife of the former president, visited Beijing in the middle of the financial crisis and told her Chinese hosts that the human rights issue should not damage trade relations between the two countries, it became obvious the balance of power had changed and that the United States was no longer in a position to extract political concessions from China. In the early 1990s, on the other hand, China sought to remake its image in the West following the Tiananmen Square crisis. It also wanted to be admitted to major international associations such as the World Trade Organization. Bill Clinton made the release of Chinese dissidents a condition of his support for the Chinese regime's international ambitions.

In the winter of 1994, the White House announced that Beijing had until June 3 to show signs of openness in terms of human rights. If not, the American government would withdraw the trade privileges that allowed China to export $30 billion a year in products to the American market. On April 24, a few weeks before the date of the ultimatum, Wang Juntao was taken to Beijing Airport and after a brief meeting with his family was put on board a United Airlines flight for New York. China announced that Wang was freed for medical reasons and would be treated in the United States. Wang Juntao was suffering from hepatitis and had heart trouble. The self-assured young intellectual from the Tiananmen Square days was but a shadow of himself. His release was seen as a major concession by China to pressure from Washington.

Less than three months later, it was Wei Jingsheng's turn to be freed and exiled to the United States, also for medical reasons. His release came two weeks after Chinese leader Jiang Zemin's visit to the United States. Wei was in terrible condition when he got off the plane in Detroit. He was taken to hospital immediately and given a battery of tests for his health problems: shingles, chronic bronchitis, high blood pressure, liver problems blamed on poor nutrition, and arthritis. Wei had spent almost all of the last seventeen years in prison, detained for some time in an unheated glass-encased cell under constant light. Other prisoners were regularly sent into the cell to beat him up. Nevertheless, he always refused any release that would not allow him to live in China. His sister, who served as his spokesperson when he arrived in the United States, said he accepted the medical exile due to his prison conditions and his state of health.

During Jiang Zemin's visit, Washington and Beijing negotiated not only the release of Wei Jingsheng but also of Wang Dan, the best-known Chinese dissident outside China. In April 1998, Wang Dan was taken from his cell in a prison in the northwest of China to Beijing and put on a plane for Detroit. His release occurred shortly before Bill Clinton's visit to China. In exchange, Washington also agreed to withdraw its support of a UN motion blaming China for its human rights record. Wang Dan also suffered from health problems, including a chronic sore throat.

The White House's strategy was to begin a constructive dialogue with China on the issue of human rights and trade. The reasoning was that it was easier to obtain concessions from Chinese leaders if there were sustained relations with them. Bill Clinton's visit to China in June 1998, eight months after Jiang Zemin's visit to the United States, aimed to seal this new relationship. But the Democrats' approach was criticized not only by many Republicans, who accused the president of being too indulgent toward an authoritarian regime, but also by human rights groups. These groups, while very pleased about the release of Wang Juntao, Wei Jingsheng, and Wang Dan, feared they could not return to China and that their voice would disappear in their American exile. Their health restored, Wang Dan and Wang Juntao resumed their studies. Harvard and Columbia universities gave them the equivalent of the status of resident dissident. They also campaigned for organizations promoting democracy in China. But their existence was essentially that of political exiles. The Chinese government had no intention of letting them return to China. When their passports expired they would not be renewed. Wei Jingsheng, the most senior of the dissidents, established a foundation in Washington for the defence of human rights in China. He still awaits the day when he can return home to a democratic China.

Bill Clinton's new doctrine toward China had serious and unexpected consequences on what remained of China's democratic movement. Many veterans of Tiananmen Square who avoided prison or completed their sentences saw the resumption of dialogue between Washington and Beijing as an opportunity to renew their struggle. They were encouraged by Jiang Zemin's speech at Harvard during his official visit to the United States. The *New York Times* reported that Jiang addressed the audience in Chinese and English and reminded them that he had visited Harvard as a young civil servant forty years earlier. He told them that even during that first trip he had understood the "general concept of democracy." Then he added, "However, during my current trip to the United States, starting from Hawaii,

I felt more specific understanding of the American democracy, more specific than I learned from books." Jiang, smiling and using humour, attached little importance to the protesters outside the building. For those who wished to believe in it, the speech of the Communist Party's general secretary and president of the People's Republic may have represented new openness of the Chinese government to the ideas of democracy and dissidence. The White House, also sensing the new tolerance on the part of the Communist leader, encouraged the Chinese to express themselves.

On June 25, 1998, taking advantage of Bill Clinton's arrival for his official visit to China, three Chinese showed up at the county seat of Hangzhou, in the east, to officially register the Democracy Party of China, which they had secretly formed. The act would test the White House's new doctrine and reveal the true nature of the Chinese president's conciliatory remarks at Harvard. One of the three men was Wang Youcai, who spent two years in prison for his role in the Tiananmen Square demonstrations. In 1989, he was on the list of twenty-one people sought by police. Addressing journalists, Wang declared he hoped Bill Clinton "would support the establishment of an opposition party in China." For that reason, he added, he and his colleagues had decided to register their party the same day the American president arrived on Chinese soil. But Wang Youcai did not manage to register his democratic party. "Local officials were confused because there was no procedure for registering a political party," he said. It didn't take long, however, for the authorities to recover. A few weeks later, Wang Youcai was arrested at his home and accused of plotting to overthrow the government.

Clinton's visit to China offered little protection to Wang or other Chinese who wanted to make their voices heard. Even before the end of his trip, Clinton's doctrine of constructive relations with China was already showing its limitations. In Xi'an, police detained an activist who announced he intended to ask Bill Clinton to meet human rights groups. Police expelled several other activists from the city. When he arrived in this city in the north of China, known for its terra cotta warriors, the president was immediately questioned by journalists accompanying him about the activist's arrest. "If it's true," Clinton declared, "it does not show China at its best, not a China turned toward the future, but one that is looking backward." The Chinese government may have increased its investments and trade with the United States and agreed to free political prisoners in exchange for symbolic concessions on the question of human rights, but on no account did it intend to open its doors to political reform. Even though Jiang Zemin said he understood American democracy better during his trip to the United States, that did not mean he wanted to import it to China. This was a hard blow for the White House. The activists' arrest occurred at the same time that the American president was inciting the Chinese government to show more openness on the issue of political reform. Clinton and Jiang may have agreed to set up a twenty-four-hour phone line as a token of better relations, but they were clearly not speaking the same language. The Americans, however, were not only angry at the Chinese authorities for humiliating the president on his first trip to China. Even if they had encouraged the Chinese dissidents to express themselves during the American president's visit, Bill Clinton's advisers now criticized Wang Youcai and the other democratic activists for having gone too far. Whether they had set themselves up for the fall was now a moot question for the activists. The Chinese regime would show them no mercy.

Six months later, in December 1998, Wang Youcai and his associate Qin Yongmin were brought before the courts. The third member of the group, Xu Wenli, awaited trial. They had no legal representation since the police had intimidated all lawyers who considered representing them. In addition to being accused of usurping the powers of state, Wang Youcai was accused of plotting with foreign enemies of China. The severe sentences handed down to Wang Youcai and the two other leaders of the Democratic Party of China — eleven, twelve, and thirteen years, respectively — dissuaded other members of the party from continuing their activities. The party was basically stillborn. "How can you recruit members in circumstances like these?" said a regional representative of the party.

The day following Wang Youcai's trial, Chinese leader Jiang Zemin made an important speech to Communist Party officials at the Great Hall of the People in Beijing. In language and tone that contrasted sharply with the apparent openness he had shown on his visit to the United States, he declared unequivocally that the Chinese political system, founded on the supremacy of the Communist Party, should not be "shaken, weakened or abandoned." The Western model, he added, "must never be copied." People who imagined that introducing a market economy in China was a prelude to importing liberal democracy were wrong, he said. He called upon all party members to be vigilant in the face of any "infiltration, any subversive or separatist activities by hostile forces, whether they be domestic or foreign in nature." The government, he declared in a final warning, would "nip in the bud" any organized attempt to oppose the Communist Party. Without naming them, he was targeting Wang Youcai and the hundreds of members of the Chinese Democratic Party who thought the ground was fertile for political plurality. The severe sentences handed down to Wang and the others a few days later left no doubt in this regard.

Six years later, in 2004, following pressure from the White House, Wang Youcai was released and exiled to San Francisco by Chinese authorities. One more transaction in the commerce of concessions between the West and China. The previous week the American government had severely criticized China's human rights record in its annual report. Beijing was also trying at the time to convince the European Union to lift its embargo on arms sales to China.

Shortly after his arrival in the United States, Wang Youcai enrolled in doctoral studies in nuclear physics. In the winter of 2009, he was completing work on his dissertation in a private laboratory in Virginia. It takes three hours to go by train from Washington to the small city where he lives and works. I was anxious to meet him to understand what motivated him to want to establish a political party that threatened the Communist Party's supremacy so soon after Tiananmen Square. Was it courage, idealism, rashness, or the martyr syndrome that led him to do something that would inevitably result in a heavy prison sentence? He had agreed to pick me up at the station. He showed up in a beat-up car. Then we drove to his laboratory. It was a Saturday, and no one was there. At forty, Wang Youcai felt a sense of urgency. He was eager to live a more normal life with his wife, who worked in New York's financial district. He felt embarrassed to still be in school at his age, and was working twice as hard to make up for lost time and finish his doctorate. He is small, nervous man with a high-pitched voice and hesitant English who lives alone in a small apartment and cooks all his meals. He was not yet used to American food. He told me he was convinced he was being watched by Chinese government agents.

If he tried to start the Chinese Democratic Party, register it with local authorities, and have it recognized legally, he tells me, it was because he does not consider himself a radical. "I wanted to go gradually," he continues, "because if you act abruptly in China, it doesn't work." He of course was remembering Tiananmen. "But you were still one of the student leaders in 1989," I reminded him. "Not really," he replied. He said he mostly took care of logistics, finding volunteers to ensure the demonstrations ran smoothly. When things heated up, he says, he advised students to tell the police he had recruited them, to protect them. That is how he found himself on the list of the twenty-one most wanted. He was on the run for two months before his arrest.

Nine years later, when he took advantage of Bill Clinton's visit to try to register his new party with the municipal secretariat in Hangzhou, he did not expect to succeed. "If you want to agree to register the party, that's fine," I told the party officials. "If not, it doesn't matter." For Wang Youcai, the important thing was the act, however symbolic. "I had the right to make the gesture and they had the right to refuse it. I told myself if we began to familiarize the Communist Party with democracy, one day we could move forward." Yet he had misread the political winds and would pay for it dearly. During his trial, he conducted his own defence. He argued that his political activities were legal in accordance with the Chinese constitution and an international treaty on political and civil rights that China had just signed. To no avail; the fix was in. The judge interrupted him before he even finished his plea. His wife, one of the few people allowed in court, timed the session. The trial had lasted two hours and ten minutes.

After our meeting, Wang Youcai drove me back to the station. I came to the conclusion that he was at once lucid and idealistic, rash and cautious, as paradoxical as it may seem. He insisted on waiting for the train with me, in a small lobby. He spoke loudly, like many Chinese, which irritated one woman who kept giving him looks. He didn't notice. Of all the Chinese dissidents in exile whom I met, he was definitely the one who seemed the most lost in the America that gave him asylum.

★ ★ ★

Wang Youcai and the hundreds of other members of the Chinese Democratic Party are part of a long line of Chinese who, since the end of the nineteenth century, deem that the cause of democracy in China is important enough to devote their lives to it. Wang's attempt to have his party officially recognized was short-lived, and he ended up paying a heavy price for it. Nevertheless, it was an important milestone in China's struggle for democratization. Wang hoped to advance the cause of democracy, to build on earlier campaigns, including Tiananmen, for which he had gone to prison. There had been the Hundred Flowers Campaign, a heartfelt revolt by intellectuals victimized by the Mao machine; the Democracy Wall, the reformers' first timid foray into the streets following the Cultural Revolution; and the Tiananmen Square demonstration, a mass movement for political reform and freedom of expression. Faced with these failures, democracy activists such as Wang Youcai tried a gentler, more strategic approach, trying to have the legality of a political opposition to the Communist Party recognized. They were no more successful, but the new ways they tried to make China more democratic influenced people who, still today, fight for better governance and greater government accountability.

The 1990s saw the assertion, then the consolidation of Deng Xiaoping's economic pragmatism. Despite his withdrawal from politics, Deng remained a major influence behind Jiang Zemin's throne. Jiang, considered during most of his mandate to be a transitional leader, felt the need to refine the justification of the Communist Party's monopoly of power at a time when China was merging into an international economy governed by the rules of the market. During the party's 14th Congress in the fall of 1992, Jiang, now fully converted to Deng and his modernization program, had two important principles adopted. The first asserted that the party must set about building "socialism with Chinese characteristics." The second stated that China was now a "socialist market economy," with strong emphasis on the term *market*. Jiang was careful to have both expressions approved by Deng during a meeting at his home before submitting them to the party. These two slogans allowed China to justify drifting toward capitalism. It also allowed the party to distance itself from the Marxist-Leninist doctrine and Mao Zedong's thought.

Jiang Zemin's second achievement was his doctrine of the "three represents." Essentially, he asserted that the Communist Party had to represent three realities: advanced productive forces, China's advanced culture, and the fundamental interests of Chinese society. This theory of Jiang Zemin's was his intellectual legacy. It allowed the Communist Party to claim to be the only one qualified to speak for the interests of the Chinese.

Jiang's third and final initiative permitted new Chinese capitalists to become members of the Communist Party. The government feared that with a growing class of entrepreneurs, the party would be perceived as being cut off from the new Chinese reality if it did not incorporate them in its ranks. Of the many paradoxes in the Chinese landscape, this last one seems the most irreconcilable. Jiang justified the decision to give Communist Party membership cards to business people, saying they were not the predatory capitalists that Marx denounced but honest people who respected the law, did not exploit their employees, and contributed to building Chinese market socialism. Including business people in the party was tempered by the fact that, according to Communist Party credo, the market economy characterizing China today is only the preliminary stage in achieving scientific socialism.

By raising socialism to the status of science, by establishing Deng's pragmatism as a political doctrine alongside that of Marx and Mao, by writing in the constitution that only the Communist Party was capable of representing China's superior interests, Jiang Zemin tried to make any political or even constitutional opposition to the party's supremacy more difficult. But for all its declarations about the superiority of socialist democracy, the party still chooses its leadership based on principles dating from the time of Mao. It was Deng, not the People's Congress or even the politburo, who designated Jiang Zemin's successor and China's next president, Hu Jintao. When Hu became president in 2002, he represented the fourth generation of leaders since the revolution, the one that would be known as the generation of managers. He inherited a rapidly growing China, but one beginning to feel confined in the political straitjacket it had donned in the days following Tiananmen Square. Despite professing democratic faith, the Chinese government remained, at the beginning of 2000, an authoritarian regime without any real mechanism to allow its citizens to express themselves. Yet in this China of 2000, activists sought less to reshape the political system than to claim very concrete rights, rights often scorned by the courts and political authorities. At the turn of the new century, the struggle for democratization therefore became a struggle for responsible government more than for democracy, and it found new avenues to circumvent the party's barriers.

8

Han Dongfang's Perseverance

Hong Kong, May 30, 2009

As he does every morning, Han Dongfang takes the ferry from Lamma Island, where he lives, to Hong Kong, a twenty-minute trip. Once in the city, he walks through the Sheung Wan commercial district. The street is teeming with merchandise: commodities of all sorts, including snakes used for traditional medicine. The smell of dried fish reminds him of his youth in Shanxi Province, years marked by the Cultural Revolution when he remembers being constantly hungry. Han Dongfang makes his way to his office at the *China Labour Bulletin*, located in a former factory, and there, step by step, he sets about building democracy in China. Not democracy with a capital D, with its political parties and its right to vote, but a democracy of rights, a useful, practical democracy for the workers of the new industrial China.

We are only a few days away from the anniversary of Tiananmen Square, and activists in Hong Kong are preparing to hold a huge demonstration against the Chinese Communist regime. But Han Dongfang will not attend. This veteran of Tiananmen Square, who spent twenty-two months in prison, no longer believes in protests. "I advise people not to take to the streets," he says. "Better to go to court. Fight by using the system, not by confronting it. The streets are not a sure thing; that's the lesson I learned from Tiananmen Square." He seems like a Gandhi of organized labour. The offices of the *China Labour Bulletin*, the workers' magazine Han Dongfang founded in 1994, have all the trappings of a left-wing NGO: modest melamine furniture, bookshelves sagging under the weight of books and journals on the labour community, and paper cups for coffee.

Han Dongfang is a tall, slender man with thick hair and gentle eyes. He has undeniable charisma. He divides his days between the offices of the *China Labour Bulletin* and the radio studios of Voice of America, where he hosts a program for workers in mainland China. They are asked to tell him about their grievances, by phone or on the Internet. Han Dongfang gives them advice or refers them to lawyers who work for him in China. In the afternoon, he goes to a lunch counter in the neighbourhood where he always orders the same thing: Vietnamese beef soup. There, sitting at a Formica table, he describes his incredible odyssey and how he came to the conclusion that China's struggle for democracy needs to be progressive rather than provocative.

I n the early hours of June 4, 1989, an exhausted Han Dongfang was fast asleep in a tent at Tiananmen Square when suddenly he was awakened by a group of men who informed him the situation had become too dangerous and he had to follow them. Outside, gunfire from the advancing army could be heard. Han, twenty-five years old, was the face and voice of the workers' movement that had joined the student movement. But Han refused to leave. His life, he told them, was not worth more than anyone else's. The young men did not agree: "You are China's Lech Walesa," one of them told him, referring to the Polish labour leader who founded the Solidarity Movement. "You can't sacrifice yourself." Then they grabbed hold of him and took him away by force. They acted as personal bodyguards, protecting him from bullets. Leaving him off a few streets away to the east, near his home, they headed back to Tiananmen Square. He never knew who they were or who had sent them.

Yet Han Dongfang did not seem destined to play an important role in the events of Tiananmen Square. In 1989, he was a labourer doing maintenance on refrigerator cars on the railway. When the first student protests began in mid-April, his wife took him to see what was happening. During discussions with students, however, Han began to think about the workers' situation. "It was the first time I heard democracy discussed as an entity in itself. Until then democracy had always been incorporated into other concepts, such as 'democracy under proletarian dictatorship.' I knew of course that the Chinese word for democracy, *min zhu*, means the people are masters. I suggested we should think about what democracy meant for the workplace, such as control of management and profits." Han Dongfang then decided to found, with others, an independent workers' movement so workers' voices would be represented and heard in Tiananmen Square. When journalists asked him how many people belonged to his organization, however, he was embarrassed. Very few workers had joined his movement out of fear of reprisals: forming a labour union outside the structure of state Communist unions was illegal. Railway representatives visited him to discourage him from continuing his political action. They told him he risked not only prison but also possibly death. However, Han did not budge, quite the opposite. "I felt exalted at the idea of death," he told me. "It would even be good to die like that. Many students thought the same way. Dreams of heroism filled the air."

Be that as it may, on the morning of June 4, Han Dongfang chose to flee rather than be a martyr. Incredible as it may seem, he made it out of Beijing on a bicycle. But after wandering for a few days in the countryside without a cent, reduced to sleeping out in the open, Han decided to return to Beijing and face the consequences. He remembered the words he uttered in Tiananmen Square a few weeks before. If someone had to go to prison, he had declared, he would be the first to do so. Filled with remorse, he made the trip back, still by bicycle. He approached Tiananmen Square, where he saw the soldiers, and headed toward the Public Security Bureau. The police officer who greeted him congratulated him on turning himself in. "It will save your life," he told him. But Han Dongfang told he had not come to turn himself in because he had done nothing illegal; he had come to defend his rights under the constitution. During the following twenty-two months, authorities tried to make him sign a document acknowledging he turned himself in. He refused, although he was beaten, deprived of sleep, and subjected to long interrogations. When he was hospitalized after a hunger strike, the authorities, weary of fighting, freed him. No accusation was made against him; the state did not put him on trial. But he paid dearly for his months of imprisonment. He contracted tuberculosis. All the prisoners in his cell, he said, were spitting blood. There was no medication. An American doctor who examined him shortly after his release concluded that the disease had so affected him that one of his lungs had to be removed. In the fall of 1992, the American Federation of Labour (AFL) and the Congress of Industrial Organization (CIO), the American labour union, paid for his trip to New York. The operation took place at the Columbia University hospital.

Unlike other dissidents expelled from China, Han Dongfang did not resign himself to an exile in the United States. One year later, when he had recovered sufficiently, he headed for Hong Kong on a tourist visa. From there, he took a small boat and was dropped off on the coast of mainland China. This was the opposite journey of the one taken by the students who had managed to flee China secretly in the days following Tiananmen Square. Han intended to go to Beijing but was arrested when he stopped at a hotel in Guangzhou. The police returned him to the Hong Kong side of the bridge that linked the mainland to the British colony. After a few more unsuccessful attempts to enter mainland China, Han Dongfang realized his mission in life was not to continue annoying the Chinese government by trying to cross the border but to create a workers' movement in China. That was something he could work at from Hong Kong. So he founded the *China Labour Bulletin,* a journal with a Mandarin edition that he mails to ten thousand factories in China each month, as well as an English edition that aims to inform the rest of the world about the problems of Chinese workers. "I was aware that in many cases the journal ended up in factory management offices or police stations, but I told myself maybe it helped educate the bosses and the police officers," he says with a touch of irony.

Ever since, with the help of his journal and radio program, Han Dongfang has been informing Chinese workers of their rights and the most effective ways to defend them. He wants to break the vicious cycle of local workers' demonstrations and revolts that usually lead to the labour leaders' arrest but produce little gain for the workers. He encourages factory workers who feel cheated to use the courts. He teaches them how to hold union elections that will allow them to democratically replace the workers' representatives tied to the party and company management. Beijing lawyers are sent to the area of the labour dispute to help the workers. "Since all this is based on a solid legal foundation," Han explains, "the police often do not dare crack down on workers. If you have a significant number of workers who show solidarity and file a complaint, it is difficult for the courts to pass judgments that go against the laws of the country. We all know, of course, that it happens."

The workers' fear of reprisals, however, is hard to overcome. "The Chinese experienced the Cultural Revolution and the Tiananment crackdown of June 4, 1989, then after June 4, it was the great darkness," says Han Dongfang. "They are afraid but can't explain why. There is no worse fear than the one you can't explain. When you know the reasons of your fear, you can act. By giving legal assistance to workers, we help them understand there is no reason to be afraid." For Han Dongfang, each victory in a village, in a factory, is one more step toward building a democratic China.

★ ★ ★

The path Han Dongfang has chosen reveals how much things are changing in China but also how, in other respects, they remain the same. The battle waged by Han Dongfang, the trade unionists, and lawyers sensitive to the workers' cause is fought on another ground than that of the traditional fight for democracy, namely the people's right to elect its government. Activists such as Han Dongfang strive for what today are commonly called "citizens' rights." These are rights not necessarily recognized by charters of universal rights, but they are essential for the greater democratization of China and especially for a better quality of life. Here we are talking about the right to fair working conditions, drinking water, education, and health. For the great majority of Chinese, these are the most important rights, more essential for the moment than freedom of speech or the right to vote.

That does not mean that activists such as Han Dongfang have abandoned the objective of a democratic system. Quite the opposite. But they believe that for China's democratization to be successful, it first needs a civil society, the rule of law, and a social contract. These will help create the preconditions for a viable democracy. The memory of the failure of the Tiananmen Square movement is central to their thinking. So is the democratic setback in Russia and in many countries of the former Soviet Union. For activists such as Han Dongfang, a functional democracy involves much more than just holding elections. There is a fundamental difference between democracy, which remains an objective, and democratization, which is the road that leads to it. This nuance in the words and strategies used by democracy activists in China shows how much their thinking has evolved. In 1989, democracy was an ideal, a kind of impulsive rush to reform, but student leaders had thought very little about what this democracy would look like if they ever had the opportunity to implement it. It is hard to imagine how they could have led China if the Communist regime had collapsed.

The fact that a new class of qualified lawyers can now defend rights before courts that are presided over by increasingly professional judges reveals that a new framework is being created in China. It signals the beginning of a new rule of law that allows citizens who feel they have been wronged to have access to some form of justice. It is also good for Chinese authorities, who realize it is better for grievances to be settled before the courts than in the streets. In 2006, the Chinese government reported there had been no fewer than eighty-six thousand illegal protests in China in the previous year. Farmers who blamed local authorities because their land had been illegally confiscated, residents angry because they were unsuccessful in fighting the management of factories that pollute the water, citizens who no longer tolerated police brutality. That is why the government tolerates lawyers who contest the actions of local authorities. Creating a legal framework where disputes of the new market economy can be arbitrated is seen as an essential condition to the social stability of a profoundly changing China.

Chinese reformers today are concentrating on advancing citizens' rights also because it is the only avenue open to them. The prospects for political democratization are as distant as ever, so they keep on fighting where they can. Anyone daring to venture into forbidden territory by claiming human rights or liberal democracy, however, is liable to severe reprisals. One of the most striking cases is certainly that of Hu Jia, an activist who served a three-and-a-half-year prison sentence for daring to criticize the Communist Party.

Hu Jia represents a new generation of activists called cyber-dissidents. In 1989, he was only sixteen. For him, Tiananmen Square is a teenage memory. It's the aberrations and injustices of the new capitalist China that made him an activist. At university, he majored in computer science, but in his free time pursued interests in environmental issues, two new realities of contemporary China. At the end of the 1990s, Hu became an activist for a variety of causes. Then a friend told him of the victims of blood contaminated by the AIDS and hepatitis viruses in southern China. Hu Jia became their staunchest defender. He made repeated representations to the authorities to obtain compensation for them. His work earned him national notoriety in the early 2000s. Hu Jia also knew the power of the Internet. He had a blog where the Chinese could share complaints. A blog that had become, in a way, a new virtual letter box for citizens' grievances. Hu was soon considered the Robin Hood of the Chinese Internet.

Gradually, from his computer station, Hu Jia tested the limits of the Communist regime's tolerance. The line to cross, however, was not clear. The laws on subversion, the ones usually cited at dissidents' trials, are deliberately vague, which gives state prosecutors a great deal of latitude. Hu Jia proceeded gradually. In the beginning, in addition to the victims of HIV-contaminated blood, he defended farmers who had been illegally expropriated and people who complained that companies were polluting their environment. Over time, however, Hu Jia's criticism became more and more focused on the very nature of the political regime. He concluded that the source of all these grievances was the authorities' lack of accountability. In a particularly harsh article, he told how police tortured two people protesting against the illegal seizure of their home in Beijing. And he didn't stop there. He criticized the government's human rights record and launched petitions demanding the release of political prisoners. In doing so, Hu Jia crossed into forbidden territory by criticizing the nature of the regime itself, not just its officials.

In 2006, the police placed him under house arrest. But far from ceasing his campaign for rights, he used the Internet to circumvent the constraints of his physical detention. He blogged constantly and produced a documentary on his detention. With his small video camera, he captured images of the police harassing his wife when she tried to leave the building where they live. The documentary is called *Prisoners in Freedom City*. Freedom City is the name of their housing complex. In the fall of 2007, Hu decided to take advantage of the upcoming Olympics to step up his campaign. He testified by videoconference before a committee of the European parliament inquiring into human rights violations in China. For the Chinese regime, that was the last straw. On December 27, Hu Jia was arrested. The police cut the Internet connection and telephone line in his home. In March, he was brought before the courts with accusations of trying to usurp state powers and of wanting to overthrow the Communist regime. Specifically, he was charged with publishing articles critical of China abroad and for giving interviews to foreign journalists. What seemed to offend the government most was an article in which Hu Jia accused Chinese leaders of not honouring their commitment to respect human rights in exchange for getting the Olympics. His trial, in March 2008, lasted only four hours. Neither his lawyers nor his wife, Zeng Jinyan, were allowed into court.

Hu Jia's sentence of three and a half years in prison was intended as a signal to Chinese bloggers that the government would not tolerate any questioning of its legitimacy or even its actions. And with cause. The arrival of cyber-dissidents like Hu Jia in the public arena upset the unwritten agreement that existed between the government and Chinese activists since the Tiananmen crisis. The implicit rule seemed to be: authorities tolerate certain criticism providing it is made in private, but as soon as its instigator decides to spread it to a group, the hammer drops. Not only do the activist bloggers violate this tacit agreement, but they do so on the Internet, a new space much more difficult for authorities to control. Monitoring the activities of well-known dissidents is relatively easy when they are limited to physical movement, the exchange of documents, telephone conversations, or meetings in cafés. Yet the arrival of the Internet poses a whole new challenge. It allows for setting up almost instantaneous virtual networks. When a dissident puts a text online or launches a petition, he has time to reach hundreds of thousands of people before the authorities manage to suppress that action. The government was fully aware of this danger when it considered allowing the Internet into China. In the end, it opted to let it in because banning the internet would have interfered with business and harmed Chinese companies in their relations abroad.[1]

Control and monitoring of the Internet require considerable resources and Herculean efforts on the part of Chinese authorities. The state created a cyber-police who, according to certain estimates, may have up to fifty thousand agents. They are in charge of monitoring everything said and written on the web. Internet cafés are required to install cameras to identify their clients. People are not allowed to use terminals in cafés anonymously: they must identify themselves to the employees when they enter. Authorities are not only on the lookout for subversive activities but have set up a filtering device allowing them to block access to foreign sites as well as any information searches deemed harmful to China's interests. Thus, searches for topics such as democracy, Tibet, or the Tiananmen Square massacre are automatically blocked. This censorship led to Google's decision to close its English-language search engine in China in the winter of 2010, a decision that leaves the field open to Chinese search engines that have no qualms about submitting to state censorship. Chinese web surfers outdo themselves in ingenuity to avoid censorship. For example, they use May 35 rather than June 4 to refer to the anniversary of Tiananmen Square. But overall the Chinese cyber-police manage to control much of what circulates.

Activists are not the only threat to the state in the virtual world of the Internet and wireless devices. So are ordinary Chinese, who use the web and their phones to state their grievances. When a national crisis arises, such as during the scandal of the melamine-tainted milk that led to the deaths of several infants and made thousands of other children sick in the fall of 2008, the Chinese used the Internet to share their anger or exchange information. Blogs or sites created especially for these occasions usually have a lifespan of a day before the cyber-police neutralize them. When the citizens of Xiamen, in the south of China, used text messaging to organize a protest against the building of a chemical factory, their campaign managed to halt the project. The organizers of this citizens' movement were nevertheless identified through their phone records and arrested. At a time when cellphones allow people to capture images of an event and transmit them thousands of kilometres away, it is becoming increasingly difficult for the Chinese government to suppress reports of protests and the spread of these outside China. During the Tibet riots in the winter of 2008, the army's surrounding of the territory could not stop Tibetans from transmitting images to the entire world through cellphones and the Internet. Following this uprising and more recent riots in the Muslim province of Xiangjiang, the popular video sharing sites YouTube, Facebook, and Twitter were blocked in China. At the beginning of the second decade of the twenty-first century in China, the Chinese government finds itself in a situation where it must not only protect its political model from being challenged by dissidents but also counter the pervasive influence of new means of communication.

This kind of censorship does not necessarily mean that Communist leaders' thinking and discourse on the question of democracy have not evolved since Tiananmen Square. In their speeches, Chinese leaders speak openly of democracy. In an address to the party congress in 2007, for example, Hu Jintao used the word *democracy* no less than sixty-one times. He even described democracy as a common objective of humanity. The democracy Hu Jintao was talking about, however, has nothing to do with Western democracy. It is a democracy practised under the Communist Party's monopoly of power. The Communist Party's analysis of its role in history remains in Mao and Deng's line of reasoning. The Communist Party is the incarnation of the democratic will of the Chinese people. This legitimacy is founded on the revolution that allowed China to free itself from the domination of foreign powers and their agents in the country, primarily Chiang Kai-shek's Kuomintang. This principle is written in the Chinese constitution. Anyone who casts doubt upon it is guilty of crimes against the state and the Chinese people. In accordance with this reasoning, activists for liberal democracy are accused of attempting to usurp the powers of state when they appear in court.

Does this mean that, in private, Chinese leaders do not wonder about democracy and how it might develop in China? Not necessarily. But they rarely give interviews on the topic or stray from party orthodoxy in their public declarations. That is why when Yu Keping (a young intellectual reportedly close to president Hu Jintao) published an essay entitled *Democracy Is a Good Thing* in 2006, several sinologists saw in it a sign that Chinese leaders were changing direction in terms of political reform. In his text, which he subsequently developed into a book published in English in the United States, Yu explains that China is on the road to "progressive democracy." He maintains that the development of democracy must be done in an orderly fashion, respecting the law and the stability of society.[2] Yu believes there are three roads that would allow Chinese citizens to participate more in political life. Democracy would first progress from the local level to higher levels of government, from inside the party toward society, and from a limited level of competition among candidates inside the Communist Party to a wider level of competition. Yet Yu does not specify the time frame for such a progressive democracy, and we don't know to what extent his views reflect those of Chinese leaders. Former president Hu Jintao and Premier Wen Jiabao spoke regularly of China's need to improve its democracy, a pledge that was also made by China's new president, Xi Jinping, when he succeeded Hu in the fall of 2012. But for many experienced sinologists, these declarations remain in line with Mao's thought.[3]

Once a year foreign journalists posted in Beijing have an opportunity to see the democracy of the Communist Party at work. In March, in the Great Hall of the People's Palace, on the left side of Tiananmen Square, delegates of the People's Congress assemble for the annual session of the Parliament of the People's Republic of China. More than three thousands delegates from all over China converge on Beijing for the Communist Party's yearly event. The party leaders take their places on the platform of the Great Hall of the People built in Soviet style in the wake of the revolution. Beautiful sprays of flowers adorn the stage. Many delegates wear the green military uniform of the People's Army; others, including those from Tibet and Xinjiang, are dressed in their national costume, colourful clothing from the high steppes that contrasts with the suits and ties of delegates from the rest of China. For the approximately ten days the event lasts, they ratify the decisions of the Communist leaders for the year to come, most of the time by unanimous vote.

These scenes are often presented in the West as a parody of democracy. The Chinese government is not insensitive to these criticisms. In 2005, it published an official document (a white paper) in which it presented its vision of what it calls a democracy with Chinese characteristics. Its primary principle is that Chinese democracy is a democracy of the people practised under the leadership of the Communist Party. "Without the Communist Party," the document says, "there would be no new China. Nor would there be people's democracy. This is a fact that has been borne out by history."[4] The corollary of this principle, according to the document, which, incidentally, is easily accessible on the government's website in many languages, is "democratic centralism." It consists, under the Communist Party's leadership, of gathering the opinions and wishes of the people and transforming them into collective decisions. The government has a duty to consult with the eight political associations grouped under the names of "democratic parties." These, recognized in the days following the revolution as allies of the Communist Party in the struggle against imperialism, include the Democratic League of China, founded in 1941, and the Chinese Peasants' and Workers' Democratic Party. It is understood that this "group of eight" do not serve as opposition to the government, as in Western-type democracies, but act as advisers in building socialism. They are considered close friends of the Communist Party of China and cooperate with them in the affairs of state. In fact, these eight political parties have little influence on the government. The people are represented by their congress, which meets once a year to ratify the government's decisions. But in no case, according to the government's official view, should a Chinese citizen place his own will above that of the collective interest. "The practice of democratic centralism also requires that the majority be respected while the minority is protected. We are against the anarchic call for democracy for all."[5]

Under Hu Jintao's presidency, the Chinese government did for the political system what Deng Xiaoping did for the economy. If Deng managed to justify introducing a market economy by describing it as socialism with Chinese characteristics, Hu justified maintaining the one-party regime by calling it a democracy with Chinese characteristics. By developing a typically Chinese model of democracy, the Communist leaders can counter criticism from abroad while telling the Chinese they are living in a democracy, no matter what the rest of the world or the dissidents say. It is well known that whoever defines the terms of a discussion holds considerable power; by defining what democracy is in China and suppressing any competing definition of the term, the Chinese government makes sure what little discussion it tolerates on political reform happens inside the parameters of the Communist Party's monopoly of power.

Communist leaders are nevertheless aware that the Chinese model faces huge problems and that the government must be more attentive to the Chinese if it hopes to maintain its legitimacy and its hold on power; it must, in other words, find a way to be more accountable for its actions. The combination of unelected officials, a new class of entrepreneurs, and the absence of a functional rule of law has led to endemic corruption in China, which in former president Hu Jintao's own words posed the most pressing threat to the Communist Party's survival. The government started building a kind of rule of law, by adopting, among other things, laws on working conditions and on the right to own property. More and more judges have legal training and are gradually replacing magistrates drawn from the ranks of the military whose mandate was to apply party justice. However, if the Chinese government wants citizens to have legal avenues to assert their rights, this desire seems limited to ensuring that the Chinese economic model operates smoothly. While in terms of social stability it is important for the Chinese to be able to address the courts to settle their differences, to assert what we could call everyday rights, the authorities draw a line when it comes to fundamental rights such as freedom of speech or of association. The government's message in this respect could not have been clearer when in the summer of 2009 it suspended the licences of three hundred Beijing lawyers specializing in human rights issues, among them the lawyer who represented cyber-dissident Hu Jia during his trial. That led many experts to say that China perhaps has a constitution guaranteeing fundamental freedoms but it has no constitutionalism allowing these rights to be applied. According to American jurist Jacques DeLisle, a renowned expert on Chinese law, Hu Jintao's desire to reform the Chinese legal system was not based on the intention to develop democracy, quite the opposite. For Hu and other Chinese leaders, argues DeLisle, the development of the law and legal processes were actually meant to provide "substitutes for democracy" and to "dampen or delay demand for democratization."[6]

For Chinese leaders, there is no paradox, because exercising personal rights cannot be done at the expense of the collective good. Under Hu Jintao, this principle stemmed not only from Mao's doctrine but also from a rich Confucian tradition that has evolved into a social philosophy, a kind of code of civil conduct. Hu Jintao's great contribution to the doctrine of the Communist Party was the concept of the harmonious society. This is a vague principle that implies the first duty of every Chinese is to work at maintaining social harmony, even at the expense of personal interests and rights. It is striking to realize how much the expression has become part of the collective imagination and everyday vocabulary. A taxi driver has only to sound his horn or cut someone off for people to say his behaviour is not harmonious.

The slogan of a harmonious society becomes an instrument that allows Chinese authorities to contain any outbreak that could negatively affect

China in times of social crisis. When the Sichuan earthquake occurred in 2008, the government reserved the right to determine what constituted harmonious behaviour among the earthquake victims. Chinese authorities were keen to show the world the image of a country afflicted by the tragedy where soldiers rescued disaster victims and the people of faraway provinces gathered supplies and foods for them. But as soon as parents of schoolchildren who had died when poorly built schools collapsed began to demand justice, the police stepped in to silence them. Such criticism of the authorities did not conform to the image of a harmonious society afflicted by mourning and tragedy. Hu Jintao's harmonious society is to some extent a softer version of the political straitjacket Deng Xiaoping imposed on China. Not only does it prohibit people from asserting their rights, but it also aims to make anyone tempted to do so feel guilty.

Hu's last important contribution to the body of Chinese Communist thought was the concept of "scientific development." Basically, he believed that technical rather than ideological solutions must be applied to China's contemporary problems. In other words, an objective, scientific approach must be developed to tackle problems such as pollution or the redistribution of wealth. Hu Jintao first brought up this principle of scientific development in 2003. Subsequently he gave the Communist Central Party School the task of defining its theory. The politburo, the nine men who led the Chinese government, adopted the principle in 2005.[7] This idea that society's problems must be settled scientifically is a distant cousin of the notion of technocratic governance in Western countries. But it also has a distinct political dimension. It has the advantage of short-circuiting any criticism of the government, since challenging the decisions of the Communist Party amounts to denying the existence of science. According to this reasoning, any call for political or economic reform violates the idea of a harmonious society and constitutes heresy in terms of scientific governance.

The Chinese government had the opportunity to demonstrate the effectiveness of its democratic model during the 2008-2009 financial crisis. At the time, China was dealing with the unexpected shock of the world financial meltdown that was throwing millions of factory workers in the south of the country out on the streets. Riots broke out in Guangzhou and neighbouring factory cities when workers, most of them migrants from Sichuan or other poor provinces, found the doors of their factories shuttered and faced employers who refused to give them their back pay. They were left with no money, no hope, no home, and nothing to lose: an explosive combination for any government. So the premier, Wen Jiabao, took advantage of the People's Congress, held in March 2009, to announce a $600 billion economic stimulus program to stop the economic hemorrhaging and put the Chinese back to work, a task made easier by the fact that he didn't have to deal with opposition in parliament or in the street.

In his speech to delegates, the premier said the party and the government needed to be more attentive to citizens in order to better respond to their expectations and grievances. But as he was saying these words, hundreds of Chinese who had come to Beijing to air their grievances were arrested and thrown into black jails, secret prisons run by the police. After a few days, they were taken to their respective villages under police escort. The People's Congress's display of unanimity and unity could not completely mask the contradictions and tensions of the new China. Even so, Chinese leaders had the leeway to fund China's response to the financial crisis without going through long debates that in Western democracies paralyzed or at least slowed down governments' efforts to get their own economic stimulus plans approved. The financial crisis allowed Chinese leaders to take comfort in the superiority of their model based on the supremacy of the Communist Party and scientific governance, a system that has the added advantage of not having to deal with the unruly idea of an elected political opposition.

In case any activist hoped to use the latent social unrest to push for reforms, the Chinese authorities also used the People's Congress in 2009 to reaffirm that China had no intention of experimenting with Western democratic political models. Wu Bangguo, the regime's second-in-command, made a harsh speech in which he said that without the absolute leadership of the Communist Party, China "would be torn by strife and incapable of accomplishing anything." The government, he added, would never agree to "hold elections among several parties or among candidates not first designated by the Communist Party." This is standard speech in party congresses. Nevertheless, the government's reaffirmation of the hard line reflected added fears in the face of economic uncertainty and of possible agitation surrounding two important anniversaries: the twentieth anniversary of the Tibetan uprising in March and of Tiananmen Square in June. The warning was specifically aimed at a group of three hundred intellectuals who felt it was the right moment to launch a campaign to demand free elections and the respect of human rights: the Charter 08 movement.

The idea of the Charter 08 movement was the brainchild of Liu Xiaobo, the same man who had negotiated the safe conduct allowing student leaders to leave Tiananmen Square peacefully in the early hours of June 4, 1989. Liu served time in prison for his role in the events of Tiananmen Square. At the time, the literary critic had returned from New York, where he taught at Columbia University, to witness the unprecedented democratic liberation movement. Upon his release from prison, Liu continued to campaign to defend human rights. He belongs to the nucleus of diehards fighting for democracy in China. His political activism has led him to be regularly arrested and imprisoned, yet the poems he wrote in prison made him internationally renowned. He served as president of the Chinese committee of PEN International, the writers' association that campaigns for the release of political prisoners.

In 2008, the Olympic year, Liu Xiaobo believed the climate was right for Chinese democracy activists to take dramatic action and relaunch the debate on democratizing the country. With the help of other dissidents such as Bao Tong, Zhao Ziyang's former right-hand man still under house arrest, Liu Xiaobo hatched the idea of a charter demanding the respect of rights and free elections. The Charter 08 movement was inspired by Charter 77, the movement launched by Vaclav Havel that led to the fall of the Communist regime in the former Czechoslovakia. Liu recruited three hundred intellectuals ready to sign the charter. It was slated to be published on December 10, 2008, a date that coincided with the sixtieth anniversary of the Universal Declaration of Human Rights. Rather than circulate a printed document, Liu and his colleagues intended to launch the Charter 08 movement on the Internet, to make it more widely available throughout China. But on December 9, on the eve of the launch, a dozen police officers stormed Liu's apartment and arrested him. They also took away three laptop computers. Liu's colleagues, however, still managed to put the charter on the Internet. Thousands of people committed themselves to supporting it before authorities managed to halt its circulation.

Few of those who signed the charter believed it would lead Liu Xiaobo to prison. After all, it did not call for the abolition of the Communist Party. It merely proposed elections in which other political parties could run against the Communists. However, the Chinese government was no more ready to tolerate such a proposal than it had been ever since the foundation of the republic in 1949. After being held more than six months in a secret location, in June 2009 Liu Xiaobo was accused, as so many others had been before him, of attempting to usurp the powers of state. He had asked for elections; he was accused of wanting to overthrow the Communist regime. He was sentenced to a heavy eleven-year prison sentence. The verdict was handed down on December 25; Chinese authorities were counting on the fact that most foreign journalists stationed in Beijing were away for the Christmas holiday.

★ ★ ★

Today the Chinese government is no more inclined to allow conflicting opinions to be expressed on the issue of political reform than it was in the days following Tiananmen Square. The suppression of the campaign in favour of the Charter 08 movement illustrates how the fight for liberal democracy in China is fought over and over, without apparent progress. When Liu Xiaobo was awarded the Nobel Peace Prize in the fall of 2010, it only deepened the divide between China and Western countries on the question of democracy and rights. It's a scenario that has been played out many times since the first democratic activists, at the end of the nineteenth century, tried to convince the court of Empress Cixi to accept the idea of a constitutional monarchy.

From his vantage point in Hong Kong, Han Dongfang is well aware he is not the first Chinese exile to try to transform China from the former British territory. A hundred years earlier, Sun Yat-sen himself had tried to organize resistance to the imperial regime of the Qing from Hong Kong. Han Dongfang also knows he may be accused, in certain circles, of playing into the hands of the Chinese government by encouraging Chinese workers to negotiate rather than protest, that he may be, inadvertently, promoting the regime's idea of harmonious society, a concept used to camouflage the conflicts in Chinese society and make any challenge to the established order seem illegitimate.

Han Dongfang does not agree with this analysis. China, he says, has a long history of social revolt. "But what did it lead to?" he asks. What China lacks, Han believes, is a rule of law — the key that would allow the door of democracy to slowly open. "That's what we are trying to do: resolve social problems through the legal system. We could call that a kind of cultural project to encourage people to trust the negotiation," he tells me. "This confidence in the legal system is essential to the development of our country."

Han Dongfang believes the first signs of this evolution are beginning to appear. China has adopted a labour code that governs working hours, conditions for dismissal, and safety criteria: new legal provisions that labour lawyers can argue before the court. Han Dongfang does not credit Chinese authorities for these improvements in legislation. "What will lead the government to be more responsible," he tells me, "is not the government. That has never occurred in the history of the world. People have to be more confident and push; that is what is happening in China. With time, the Chinese government will have no choice but to change, to become a more responsible government." For Han Dongfang, in fact, the path to victory is rarely conventional, not for the cause he defends nor for himself. Rather than stubbornly try to enter China secretly, he simply waited for China to come to him. With the handover of Hong Kong to Communist China in 1997, Han Dongfang automatically became a Chinese citizen again, a personal victory that serves as a symbol for all his action.

"And when will democracy occur?" I ask him.

"I don't have a time frame and I have no definition of democracy," Han Dongfang replies. "But I have a benchmark that will allow me to determine if China is more democratic. If 30 per cent of Chinese workers have the right to elect their own representatives and negotiate labour contracts, even with the Communist Party in power, China will be an established democracy."

It is four o'clock, but Han Dongfang's workday is far from over. Later, in the evening, he will take the ferry to return home, convinced he has advanced ever so slightly the cause of Chinese workers and democracy as he conceives it, perhaps not an ideal form of democracy but the only one possible for the moment in mainland China.

9
Xi Jinping's China

Beijing, February 27, 2011

Fearing a repetition of the protests shaking the Arab world, Chinese authorities have cordoned off the Wangfujing commercial district, not far from Tiananmen Square. On the Internet, activists are urging the Chinese to go over to the popular pedestrian mall and express their demands for reform. The same invitation applies to a dozen other cities in China. But on this sunny Sunday afternoon, there won't be any gatherings like those in Tunisia and in Egypt that triggered the fall of authoritarian regimes. Hundreds of police officers are blocking the access to Wangfujing Street. They've unwound dozens of metres of yellow tape to discourage passersby from approaching. Such a police operation may seem excessive. Very few Chinese would dare take to the streets to demand the end of the Communist regime. But authorities are nonetheless worried about any public gathering a few days before the opening of the People's Congress. Already hundreds of activists likely to cause problems for the regime have been detained or told not to leave their homes. Except for a few curious people, there are mostly police officers and foreign journalists on Wangfujing Street. Like many other correspondents, that same morning I received a phone call from Chinese authorities telling me not to attempt to cover the announced protest. I go there anyway and try to force my way through the web of side streets that lead to the meeting place of the cyber-dissidents, but the police prevent me from passing. At the southern entrance to the square, things start to get heated. Plainclothes police officers prevent camera operators from foreign television networks from filming, even though there are no protesters. A few are roughed up and detained. The following week, the Chinese government threatens to deport journalists who persist in wanting to cover any protest. Doing so would make us guilty of complicity with the people who want to overthrow the Chinese regime.

There was no democratic spring in China in 2011. The Chinese, unlike the Arab peoples, weren't hungry for revolution. China had just overtaken Japan as the second-largest economic power in the world; most Chinese were busy trying to get ahead in China's booming economy. State television did show images of what was going on in Tunisia and Egypt, but it was to remind people how demonstrating for democracy means violence and instability. Very few Chinese were aware that some Arab demonstrators invoked the memory of Tiananmen Square as a source of inspiration. Certainly they were not told that on television. More than twenty years after China underwent its own spring revolution, the memory of Tiananmen Square seems to have dissolved in time.

In the days following the Tiananmen massacre, however, history seemed to be on the side of those who believed China's democratization was only a question of time. The international context was certainly pointing in that direction. The USSR had collapsed like a house of cards; its socialist model was in ruins. In the Eastern bloc countries, people took to the streets to celebrate their new freedom and demand elections. In the spring of 1989, China seemed resolutely engaged in the same movement. Hundreds of thousands of Chinese, inspired by what they saw in the Soviet republics, braved the Communist regime and demanded reform. In this context the suppression of the Tiananmen movement appeared as a temporary failure, a first missed opportunity with democracy. Pursuing economic reforms would surely bring Chinese leaders to open the door to democratization. Democracy would naturally sprout from the fertile soil of the market economy.

The thrust of Western diplomacy after Tiananmen Square was to encourage China on this path, through cultural exchanges, economic agreements, and political pressure. According to this reasoning, granting the Olympics to China and admitting China into the World Trade Organization would progressively bring the Chinese government in tune with the West. The new Chinese entrepreneurs would gradually demand laws to protect and regulate property rights. What happened in Europe at the time of the

Industrial Revolution would also happen in China: the new capitalist economy would require impartial courts to arbitrate commercial rights and political representation to defend and promote them. Democratization would be accelerated by a global context imposing obligations on China by virtue of the economic treaties it signs. In other words, from the moment China agreed to play according to the rules of international business, it was bound to adopt a political system consistent with these rules.

Clearly this has not happened. Moreover, surveys conducted among Chinese entrepreneurs reveal that a large majority of them are adapting very well to the single-party system and do not want the Chinese to elect their government from among several political parties.[1] In fact, more and more of these Chinese entrepreneurs have joined the Communist Party since they were granted the right to do so. This convergence of interests between the business class and the political elite is reinforced by the fact that they often belong to the same families. A significant portion of the wealth in China and many state enterprises are in the hands of members of the Communist Party or their families. Former president Hu Jintao's son, for instance, founded one of the biggest security systems in the country. Former premier Wen Jiabao's son manages one of China's most important investment funds. It is understood that foreign investors who want to have access to important Chinese business circles should operate through this kind of fund. In the new China, the fact that Hu and Wen are the capitalist children of former Communist leaders seems completely natural.

Village elections, introduced in 1989, are another litmus test of China's democratic development. These have often been presented as the first step toward a progressive democratization of the entire political system. Once accustomed to electing village leaders, the Chinese would be ready to elect county officials, regional governors, and finally their parliament and their president. Yet recent studies show that the opposite is occurring. With few exceptions, far from enhancing local democracy, village elections only reinforce the Communist Party's hold over the rural areas. Some academics even claim that village elections were instituted by Chinese leaders to rebuild the credibility of local officials and prevent the "advance of formal democracy at the national level."[2]

Does this mean that Deng Xiaoping was right, that a market economy operating within the constraints of a political straitjacket is the winning formula for China? One may be tempted to believe so in light of China's extraordinary economic renaissance. China, since Tiananmen Square, has demonstrated it can straddle political authoritarianism and a market economy, that a government that calls itself Communist can, in other words, manage a capitalist economy and not collapse under the weight of this apparent contradiction.

There are very specific reasons why China has been able to stay on this course. Starting in 1989, Chinese leaders drew different conclusions than leaders of Western countries on the failure of Soviet Communism. The Chinese attributed the collapse of the USSR and its empire not so much to its unsustainable economic model as to the errors of Soviet leaders. Privately, many accused Mikhail Gorbachev of deliberately scuttling the Soviet Union and betraying the great Communist family. Experts in the Chinese government's think tanks spent a lot of time analyzing what occurred in Eastern Europe. They identified three reasons for the collapse of the Soviet system: the people's economic discontent, a lack of unity among Communist leaders, and the influence of the West.[3] Based on this analysis, the Chinese Communist party adopted vigorous measures to avoid suffering the fate of its Soviet cousin. After some initial hesitation, Deng Xiaoping managed to convince the party to speed up economic reforms in order to eliminate discontent among the people. Communist leaders also made sure to suppress any dissent within their ranks. The dismissal of Secretary General Zhao Ziyang and the heavy prison sentence imposed on his assistant, Bao Tong, served as a warning to anyone tempted to question the party line. Finally, Chinese authorities were on the lookout for any attempts by the West to promote its political model in China. The imprisonment of activists that dared propose a form of liberal democracy—whether in a blog, charter, or by trying to have a political party recognized—still today is a testament to the Communist regime's determination to nip all discussion of political reform in the bud.

Whatever was left of a political opposition that could have rekindled the ashes of the Tiananmen movement in China has thus been neutralized. This is largely due to the Chinese government's total refusal to allow any debate on its regime's nature and legitimacy. But that's not the whole story. Part of the reason the 1989 pro-democratic movement was suppressed so easily was due to the fact that the Chinese people did not feel any deep connection with the movement, though it did receive a great deal of public sympathy. The movement was an impulsive one, with no long-term strategy —young people hoping to convince the Communist Party of the need to reform. Despite their incendiary slogans, they did not intend, nor did they have the means, to overthrow the regime. The people's frustration in the spring of 1989 in China was also radically different from that in Eastern Europe. The Chinese were not crushed under the weight of a regime that could barely manage to provide for them but rather demanded a greater share in the economic expansion that was promising to bring China out of its endemic poverty. Once the Communist regime managed to improve the quality of life of a majority of Chinese, it wiped out a large part of the motives for the discontent of 1989. Many analysts believe economic reforms in China have replaced political reforms.

That does not mean the Chinese have no grievances, far from it. But these usually are related to what we can call local injustices, and are unrelated to fundamental criticism of the regime. And they are mostly individual in nature. The thousands of Chinese who make the journey to Beijing every year to submit a petition usually have a grievance against local authorities. As in the time of the emperors, they hope the central government will make the local civil servants who poison their lives listen to reason. Except in exceptional cases such as the contaminated milk crisis of 2008, when the leaders of dairy companies deliberately added melamine to their product, causing some babies to die and leaving thousands of others sick, the Chinese people's recriminations against the authorities are not collective in nature. The government is not threatened by any organized opposition. In this context, it is not surprising that the battleground for reformers in China has gradually shifted from democracy to rights. Given the limited space open to them, many Chinese activists conclude that it is more realistic and useful in the long term to try to build a civil society than to take to the streets to demand voting rights that would remain meaningless. Their reasoning is that to achieve a functional democracy it is essential to first build a rule of law. According to this logic, democracy becomes the outcome of the reforms rather than their starting point. The thousands of lawyers and activists who work for the recognition of property rights or the right to clean drinking water, proper health care, and education are fighting for what are called "citizens' rights." These rights are seen as less threatening to the authorities because they don't question the Communist regime.

However, China's relative current stability would not be possible had the Communist Party not adapted to the new environment it helped create. Even before 1989, Deng Xiaoping had begun to justify the introduction of a market economy by calling it socialism with Chinese characteristics. Such semantic licence allowed and still today allows Chinese leaders to operate outside the confines of the Communist ideology without having to officially repudiate it. By describing Chinese capitalism as a temporary step on the path to achieving scientific socialism, Communist leaders can continually postpone the date when they must settle what seems like a fundamental paradox. This allows the Communist Party to be able to maintain its name and justify the monopoly of power it holds, despite the fact it is integrating China increasingly into a global market economy. Ultimately, this apparent contradiction seems to concern Westerners more than the Chinese, who largely profit from the Communist Party's economic pragmatism. Chinese entrepreneurs, the very ones who were supposed to launch China's course to democracy, also greatly benefit from the stability that an authoritarian government provides, as do many foreign companies operating in China.

This new Chinese model even has a name — the Beijing Consensus — and this model is beginning to inspire some developing countries who have sustained relations with China. For leaders of many African or Asian countries, the Beijing Consensus, which combines the market economy and authoritarianism, is more appealing than the Washington Consensus, which claims to be a development model based on democracy and human rights. They far prefer doing business with a government and Chinese investors who do not demand free elections than with Westerners who patronize them on the question of rights and freedoms. China's new influence beyond its borders will have an impact on the international community — an impact whose extent has only begun to be measured.

Does this mean that China will never be democratic, that the regime has been successful in its bid for authoritarianism? Not necessarily. China, despite its dazzling economic success, remains vulnerable; the Communist Party's legitimacy is not grounded in democracy in the classic sense of the term but in something more fleeting and unstable, namely its economic performance.[4] This fragile legitimacy depends on the government's ability to maintain strong economic growth. Chinese leaders are very conscious of this reality. They estimate that if the annual growth rate of the Chinese economy falls below 8 per cent, the country's stability will be in danger. Yet the Chinese model is beginning to show signs of slowdown normal for an emerging country. The government has a hard time creating enough jobs for the estimated ten million Chinese who leave the countryside for the cities each year and for the millions of young graduates of its universities.[5] Problems such as inflation and the wealth gap spawned by China's amazing economic development are catching up to it.

The Chinese government had a foretaste of this new kind of challenge in the spring of 2010 when young employees of the Honda factory in Guangzhou began striking to demand better salaries due to the increase in the cost of living. Local authorities were faced with a new generation of young people who no longer accepted their parents' poor working conditions, were no longer satisfied to assemble consumer products destined for foreign markets, and demanded the means to own them. These young people, in other words, want to do more than put together the iPods of the world;

they want to be able to buy one. In the case of Honda, the factory director, who was also the leader of the local Communist Party, only managed to pacify workers by agreeing to a 40 per cent salary increase. Such cases show the shortcomings of an authoritarian regime that denies workers the right to negotiate their working conditions through independent unions and of a system with no mechanism to arbitrate social tensions.

Such sporadic revolts do not mean the Chinese government is on the verge of collapsing. Far from it. There is an emerging consensus among experts who observe China, that says it will probably be under the aegis of resilient authoritarianism for the foreseeable future.[6] But many of these same experts also agree the Chinese model is not necessarily sustainable in the long run. Chinese authoritarianism, which is founded on the absence of accountability of its leaders, has generated an endemic corruption that is beginning to undermine its ability to govern. Already the central government does not always manage to impose its will outside Beijing, where the tentacles of local mafia reach right inside the ranks of party officials. Some sinologists even feel the Chinese model is beginning to show its limits, and unless a major political reform occurs in which the parliament, the press, and the courts are no longer subjected to the Communist Party's whims, the Chinese people's grievances and frustrations are liable to be expressed increasingly in the streets.[7] The tens of thousands of demonstrations taking place each year in China, deemed illegal by the government, attest to the lack of recourse for the Chinese to make their grievances known. The incompatibility of political authoritarianism and the Chinese market economy is becoming increasingly apparent.

Can the Communist leadership still manage to remain on its current course or will the development of a middle class with access to consumer goods and the Internet, one living in an increasingly globalized world, force it to make democratic concessions? By opening the door to more transparency in the party, especially with respect to corruption, will the government inadvertently find itself calling for greater accountability? By setting objectives regarding the environment and pollution control, won't Chinese authorities be giving ammunition to citizens' groups who dare rise up against companies that pollute the environment? Can the Communist Party preside over all these changes without renouncing its monopoly on power, without granting the Chinese more say in the country's affairs, without opening the door to some form of democracy? These are the fundamental questions of the new Chinese century. Western scenarios on how China will become democratic range from a progressive evolution in which the Communist Party accepts competition from other political parties to catastrophic hypotheses of social rebellion or the army overthrowing the government following a sudden economic crisis. Predicting China's political future, however, is as precise a science as reading tea leaves. Yet one thing seems clear: the impetus for democratization, if it occurs, will come from the Chinese themselves. The time when Western countries could influence China on this issue appears to have passed.

Western leaders have fewer and fewer means to encourage Chinese leaders to set democratic reforms in motion. Today's China is a far cry from the China of 1989 — Asia's poor relation emerging from isolation. It is the second-largest economic power in the world. In times past, the American president could get Chinese leaders to free a political prisoner in exchange for a visit to the White House. Not anymore. We need only remember that Barack Obama refused to meet the Dalai Lama before his first official visit to China to avoid offending Chinese leaders. The balance of power between the United States and China has changed, and so has the very nature of the relationship. It is odd, to say the least, that a Communist country is the United States' largest creditor. Were China to dispose of a significant portion of the hundreds of billions of dollars of the American debt it holds, it would seriously injure the United States' currency and its economy.

The question of China's democratization is thus very different today than it was in 1989, when the government itself had opened the discussion on political reform. And that is not only because China has changed but because the rush to develop has also replaced or appears at least to have diminished the desire for political reform. Furthermore, the idea of liberal democracy no longer has the same appeal it did in 1989. If students demonstrated once more in Tiananmen Square today, it is doubtful they would use an effigy of the Statue of Liberty as a symbol of their demands. In the spring of 1989, the Soviet Union was dying; democracy, for those who lived under Communism, in China as elsewhere, symbolized an ideal of liberation. Yet the last twenty years have shown that in many former Soviet Union countries, including Russia, obtaining the right to vote has not guaranteed democracy. These regimes have proven it is possible to adopt a facade of democracy with universal suffrage while maintaining intact what amounts to a one-party system. Even if no fewer than ninety countries have joined the democratic club since 1974, academics who measure these states' governance speak of a definite democratic rollback.[8] The military and political resistance the United States has encountered in Iraq and NATO has encountered in Afghanistan remind us of the extent to which liberal democracy has trouble taking hold in many non-Western cultures. Holding elections is certainly no guarantee of a functional democracy. When they look at this, Chinese leaders must feel relieved they decided not to take the road to simultaneous economic and political liberalization in 1989.

Twenty years after closing the door on political reforms during the Tiananmen Square crisis, the Chinese government has developed a counter-speech that allows it to reject criticisms on the issue of democracy. China has its own form of socialist democracy. This single-party democracy is obviously meaningless from the Western point of view. Yet in the political vacuum that is China, this definition is the only one allowed and this has consequences. The harshness with which China reacted to the Nobel Peace Prize being awarded to its most famous dissident, Liu Xiaobo, in the fall of 2010 is a good illustration of this. Liu is the activist sentenced to eleven years in prison sentence for launching the Charter 08 movement, an online petition demanding free elections and freedom of speech. By denouncing the Nobel Prize committee's choice, Chinese authorities declared they do not consider democracy and the Western conception of human rights as universal values but rather as instruments of American imperialism. The era when Chinese leaders considered liberal democracy worthy but premature for China has long passed. The Chinese government now controls the very definition of democracy and is also taking the means to cast aside any competing and above all any Western conceptions of the term. The fact that the Chinese democracy forbids any debate on the notion of what democracy is is not the least of the paradoxes of contemporary China. The debate on democracy in China has traditionally been different than in other cultures. For many Chinese thinkers and activists, democracy represented more than the right to vote or responsible government. The idea of democracy represented a form of emancipation of thought. This is why many prominent proponents of reform in China believed the Chinese were not inherently ready for democracy, that they had to undergo a period of political tutelage before being qualified to elect their government responsibly. When we study the Chinese twentieth century, we realize that most Chinese leaders, whether Republican, Nationalist, or Communist, came into power promising a form of democracy but then spent a good deal of time repudiating the idea or postponing it. For Mao and the other Communist leaders, the very notion of liberal democracy was anathema. Yet when Deng Xiaoping came to power, Communist leaders understood they had to show greater accountability: corruption and lack of transparency were threatening the very survival of the Communist Party. Deng's gamble was that the party could be accountable for its actions while maintaining the monopoly of political power. It is a challenge that Deng's successors still have not managed to meet.

Chinese leaders' inability to reduce the gap between the discourse and the reality of governance came to light again in the year preceding new President Xi Jinping's designation in 2012. The Bo Xilai Affair, as it is called, not only tainted the transfer of power but also shed light on the privileges, corruption, and power games that characterize this "red nobility," the new generation of Chinese leaders who will be in power for the next ten years.

Bo Xilai was the charismatic governor of Chongqing, the thirty-two-million-inhabitant megacity on the Yangtze. From the time he was nominated, he set out to fight corruption, proclaimed himself defender of the poor, and, in a style reminiscent of the Mao years, encouraged citizens to sing socialist hymns in public. Bo counted on his image as a dispenser of justice to build a political capital sufficient to allow him to accede to the select committee of the politburo in Beijing, the nine men who before 2012 ran the country — their number has since been reduced to seven. The son of a former revolutionary hero, he had the necessary pedigree to rise to the highest echelons of power. But everything collapsed when Bo Xilai's wife was accused of murdering a family friend, a British businessman named Neil Haywood. The investigation and trial revealed that Bo Xilai and his wife were as corrupt as the people they were fighting. Bribes, influence peddling, affairs: the list of accusations and criticisms was long. Bo was even accused of wiretapping senior party members when they passed through Chongqing.

A few months short of the election of the new politburo, the scandal caused considerable embarrassment to the Chinese political class, who quickly expelled Bo Xilai from the party. Still, for the Communist Party, Bo's fall had the advantage of removing a potential opponent of the designated president, Xi Jinping. In the Chinese press, Bo was denounced as a renegade, an ambitious politician putting his personal interests above those of the country but who was an exception, an anomaly, in the Communist leadership. Bo and his friends and family were suspected of amassing a fortune of more than $160 million. Ultimately, his expulsion was to serve as proof that the party tolerated no wrongdoing in its ranks.

In the fall of 2012, a few weeks after Bo's debacle, a *New York Times* investigation shattered this fiction. Bo and his family were not the only high-profile Communists to amass a fortune while in power. The *Times* revealed that outgoing Premier Wen Jiabao and his family had a fortune estimated at $2.7 billion. Even the premier's mother, a modest village schoolteacher, age ninety, had a portfolio of more than $120 million. It was revealed that Wen's wife had made a fortune in diamonds, his brother in water purification, and his only son had built one of the largest investment funds in China. He was also at the head of a state-owned company specializing in satellite communications. None of the assets, however, were in the premier's name. The government quickly erased any reference to the affair from the Internet.

The *Times* investigation didn't report anything strictly illegal. Wen Jiabao didn't contest the stories in the *Times*, which were based on a painstaking research of public documents, though he did threaten to sue the newspaper through a Hong Kong lawyer. But the exposé of the premier's family finances did bring to light the incestuous relationship between money and power that exists in a regime still officially singing the virtues of socialism. The princelings of the revolution who became millionaires often are from the families of the most senior Chinese leaders. In some cases, they are the children of some of the most conservative elements of the Communist regime. For example, Li Xiaolin, the daughter of Li Peng, the former premier who imposed martial law during the events of Tiananmen Square and who tried to sabotage Deng Xiaoping's economic reforms, heads China Power International, one of China's largest energy companies. Since 2010, members of the government are required to reveal to the party a list of their family members' jobs and investments, but this information remains secret. When the foreign press reported in 2010 that former vice-president Zeng Qinghong's son had bought a house worth $32 million in Australia, the information was suppressed on the Chinese Internet by the cyber-police.

While this information may appear anecdotal, it reveals a system in which the elite uses its relatives to become wealthy, one in which private entrepreneurs associate themselves with the children of political leaders to get favours, and where state companies with links to those in power secure favourable loans from banks, giving them competitive advantages that undermine the normal running of the market economy. As soon as he was elected as the new secretary general of the party in November 2012, Xi Jinping denounced the corruption plaguing the Chinese regime. Yet Xi Jinping's own family has investments worth more than $300 million dollars. His predecessor, outgoing President Hu Jintao, referred to corruption more than a dozen times in his farewell speech at the People's Congress. Premier Wen Jiabao, leaving office, notwithstanding revelations about his family's fortune, worried about the billions of dollars illegally leaving China each year. This discourse is not new. In the days following the Tiananmen Square protests, Deng Xiaoping called for public trials for hundreds of senior party officials to show the people the government was taking the question of corruption and privileges seriously.

Very little has changed since then, except that the political class continues to get rich. The fifth generation of leaders who have just taken power have no more been elected than those who preceded them. Xi Jinping was designated president by a consensus of the politburo. Xi is not a rebel. He is the son of a revolutionary hero who patiently climbed the rungs of power. He is considered part of the generation of princelings, the children of Chinese leaders who were in power at the time of Mao and in many respects consider themselves to be keepers of the legacy of the revolution. None of this predisposes Xi to contemplate radical changes.

Even if Xi Jinping turns out to be the enlightened leader that many Chinese activists dream about, he would have to undertake a major shift to launch China on the road to democratization. He would have to repudiate his predecessors' political discourse and dismantle the ideological architecture they put in place since the economic shift set in motion by Deng Xiaoping more than thirty years ago. This would mean repudiating important principles set into the Chinese constitution or that are important tenets of the Communist Party doctrine. Such a shift would imply recognizing that the Communist Party is not the only one authorized to speak on behalf of the people, its monopoly of power is not justified, the capitalist shift is not a step on the road to achieving socialism, and demanding democracy should not be a crime punishable by a heavy prison sentence. In other words, Xi would have to admit that Chinese socialist democracy is not a true democracy. He would also have to admit that the only effective way to fight the endemic corruption threatening China's future involves true accountability of its leader, namely himself — thus invoking a true form of responsible government. This would mean making public the privileges of the political class he represents and holding himself accountable to the will of the people through elections. It is hard to imagine a Chinese leader making such an about-face unless events forced him to do so.

Each generation that preceded Xi Jinping's generation's rise to power embodied a specific period in China: Mao, the Communist adventure and utopia; Deng Xiaoping, the pragmatist shift; Jiang Zemin, the consolidation of the capitalist-authoritarian model; Hu Jintao, the technocratic management of the new economy. Xi Jinping will be the first Chinese president born after the revolution or who was not part of the political structure during the events of Tiananmen Square. Many Chinese activists hope that will give him complete freedom of action to look at this crisis with new eyes, to free himself from a discourse that denies the very existence of the tragedy. For many Chinese activists, China cannot move forward on the road to political reform until it sheds the heavy legacy of Tiananmen Square. For them, a first step toward national reconciliation has to involve rehabilitating those who paid dearly for their role in the events, even all those persecuted for fighting in the name of democracy. Some exiled veterans of the fight for political reform like to say, in an irony tinged with bitterness, that while they have found a haven of freedom under foreign skies, they have lost the land of China. Reconciling heaven and earth, as we know, was the duty of ancient emperors. Any progress on political reform in today's China, however, cannot happen until Chinese leaders come to the conclusion that fundamental rights, such as freedom of expression and the right to choose one's government, are the best guarantee of China's development. Reform cannot occur until the leaders understand that the cost of taking no action is higher than the cost of change. Only then can the exiled veterans of the democratic struggles, who paid so dearly for their commitment to their ideals, hope to leave foreign soil and return to a land of freedom.

Dissidents and Political Figures

Bao Tong Right-hand man of Zhao Ziyang and responsible for the Office of Political Reform instituted by Deng Xiaoping. Considered too close to the student leaders, he was fired in 1989 and sentenced to seven years in prison. Since his release, he has been living under house arrest in Beijing.

Chai Ling Leader of the radical wing of the student movement, she is called the Joan of Arc of Tiananmen Square. In the days following the massacre, she fled Beijing and managed to reach Hong Kong in the hold of a boat. She lives in Boston, where she runs a student placement company.

Chen Zeming A Chinese intellectual and reformer and colleague of Wang Juntao, with whom he co-founded the first independent political research institute in China. Imprisoned for his support of the students, he lives in Beijing, where, since his release, he continues to fight for political reform.

Chiang Kai-shek Disciple of Sun Yat-sen, leader of the nationalist forces, this career soldier unified China under his authoritarian regime in the 1920s. Destabilized by the invasion of Japanese armies, he lost power to Mao and his Communist Revolution. Defeated, he fled to Taiwan, where he set up a parallel government to the one in Beijing.

Deng Xiaoping Veteran of the Great March and the Communist Revolution. Ousted by Mao during the Cultural Revolution, he was rehabilitated upon Mao's death and led China until the early 1990s. Instigator of the Chinese economic shift of the 1980s, Deng initiated reflection on political reform. In 1989, unwilling to accept students' demands, he ordered soldiers to crush the protest movement in Tiananmen Square.

Hu Jia Defender of Chinese victims of contaminated blood. First Chinese activist sentenced to prison for Internet activities.

Hu Jintao President and general secretary of the Communist Party from 2002 to 2012. Appointed by Deng Xiaoping. An engineer by training and a technocrat, he is responsible for the concepts of harmonious society and scientific development to justify the Communist Party's monopoly on power and dismiss any demand for democratic reform.

Hu Yaobang General secretary of the Communist Party and partisan of democratic reform in the Chinese leadership. Fired by the conservative wing of the politburo in 1987. His death in 1989 set off the protest movement in Tiananmen Square.

Jiang Zemin General secretary of the Communist Party in the wake of the Tiananmen Square crisis. A moderate conservative, he consolidated Deng Xiaoping's economic reforms and authorized membership of business people in the Communist Party.

Li Peng Premier and hard-liner against the students in 1989. Responsible for the martial law that led to the repression of the protest movement. Known in China as the "Butcher of Tiananmen Square."

Liu Xiaobo An academic and literary critic who negotiated the departure of the student leaders from Tiananmen Square. Imprisoned in the wake of the Tiananmen Square crisis, he continued to fight for political reforms upon his release. Sentenced again to prison in 2009 for launching the Charter 08 movement demanding free elections, he received the Nobel Peace Prize in 2010.

Mao Zedong Father of the Chinese Communist Revolution. Supreme leader of China from 1949 until his death in 1976. Dictator whose purges and policies caused the death of tens of millions of Chinese.

Sun Yat-sen Chinese revolutionary and reformer. Founder of the Kuomintang Party and first president of the Republic of China in 1912. Considered to be the father of modern China.

Wang Dan Iconic leader and head of the moderate wing of the Tiananmen student movement. Arrested in Beijing after a few weeks on the run, he received a heavy prison sentence. In 1997, he was exiled to the United States. He currently lives and teaches in Taiwan.

Wang Juntao Chinese intellectual and reformer. Adviser of student leaders of the Tiananmen Square movement, he was considered one of the "black hands" behind the protest movement and received a heavy prison sentence. Exiled to the United States in 1994, he works in academia in New York.

Wei Jingsheng Former Red Guard who became a political activist. Prominent member of the Democracy Wall movement in 1978, he was found guilty of treason and imprisoned twice before being exiled to the United States. He lives in Washington, D.C., where he runs a foundation dedicated to democracy in China.

Wen Jiabao Premier from 2003 to 2012. Called Grandpa Wen, he was considered the human face of the Communist regime. A master political survivor, he escaped the purge that carried away his former boss, Zhao Ziyang, in the wake of the Tiananmen Square crisis.

Xi Jinping Designated president in 2012, successor to Hu Jintao. Son of a Communist hero, he is considered to be a representative of the Communist Revolution's generation of princelings. He patiently climbed the rungs of power and is in line with the party's thinking.

Zhao Ziyang Premier, then general secretary of the Communist Party. Led the movement for political reform until he was fired on the eve of the Tiananmen massacre. Held responsible for the student turmoil, he was placed under house arrest until his death in 2005.

Acknowledgements

I would like to thank my publisher, Pierre Filion. He believed in this project and knew how to support it and guide it through to completion. I would also like to thank Leméac for committing to publish works that deal with ideas. I'm grateful to Susanne Alexander at Goose Lane for giving the book new life in an English edition and for believing that a book that deals with the idea of democracy in China still has relevance. My thanks also go to Jonathan Kaplansky for his translation.

Once again, I am indebted to my wife, Anne, and to my sons for tolerating a husband and father working "on another book." Their open-mindedness and sense of adventure made our stay in China unforgettable. We left there more united and enriched. China is experiencing one of the most spectacular transformations in history. The Chinese are adapting to these transformations with remarkable composure and tenacity. I am grateful to all the Chinese people who opened their doors to me, asking nothing in return, and who shared some moments of their lives with me. Unfortunately, confiding in a foreign journalist in China still carries risks today. Their generosity is therefore all the more admirable.

Finally, I wish to thank the Canada Council for the Arts for its research grant. Without this help, this project would never have come into being.

Notes

As this is not an academic work, I kept references to a minimum. The references I include deal with ideas, analyses, and facts attributed precisely to a specific author. I did not include references to information of a general nature and that is found in more than one text. The works I consulted in writing this book appear in the bibliography. I also had recourse to the *New York Times* Archives to report certain public events; I did not quote source articles so as to avoid weighing down the text. The responsibility for any factual errors or misinterpretations is mine.

1 Wang Juntao's Exile

1. Zhang Liang, Andrew J. Nathan, and Perry Link (eds.), *The Tiananmen Papers: The Chinese Leadership's Decision to Use Force Against Their Own People — In Their Own Words* (New York: Public Affairs, 2001).
2. Jean-Philippe Béja, "À la recherche d'une ombre chinoise : Le mouvement pour la démocratie en Chine (1919-2004)" in *L'Histoire immédiate* (Paris: Éditions du Seuil, 2004), 73.
3. Ibid., 243.
4. Ibid., 244.
5. Craig Calhoun, *Neither Gods nor Emperor: Students and the Struggle for Democracy in China* (Berkeley and Los Angeles: University of California Press, 1997), 269.

2 Sun Yat-sen's Unfinished Dream

1. Diana Lary, *China's Republic* (Cambridge: Cambridge University Press, 2007), 42.
2. Jonathan Fenby, *The Penguin History of Modern China: The Fall and Rise of a Great Power, 1850-2008* (London: Penguin Books, 2008), 120-121.
3. On the life and works of Sun Yat-sen, see Marie-Claire Bergère, *Sun Yat-sen* (Stanford: Stanford University Press, 1998).
4. Joël Thoraval, "L'appropriation du concept de "liberté" à la fin des Qing — en partant de l'interprétation de Kant par Liang Qichao" in Delmas-Marty and Will, *La Chine et la démocratie* (Paris: Fayard, 2007), 219.
5. Andrew J. Nathan, *Chinese Democracy* (Berkeley: University of California Press, 1985), 63.

6. Béja, *À la recherche d'une ombre chinoise,* 17.
7. The expression is by Anne Cheng, "Des germes de démocratie dans la tradition confucéenne," in Delmas-Marty and Will, 83-107.
8. Fenby, 35.
9. Ibid., 46.
10. Ibid., 136.
11. Ibid., 147.
12. Ibid., 143.
13. Ibid., 213.

3   Mao's Democracy

1. Michel Bonnin, "Servante, épouvantail ou déesse : la démocratie dans le discours du pouvoir et dans celui de la dissidence en Chine," in Delmas-Marty and Will, 499.
2. Fenby, 305.
3. Ibid., 496.
4. Ibid., 311.
5. Bonnin, 496.
6. Fenby, 330.
7. Bonnin, 499.
8. Fenby, 360.
9. Bonnin, 501
10. Ibid., 502.

4   Wei Jingsheng's Awakening

1. Spence, *The Search for Modern China* (New York: W.W. Norton & Company), 663.
2. Wei, *The Courage to Stand Alone: Letters from Prison and Other Writings* (New York: Penguin, 1997), 238.

3. Fenby, 537-538.
4. Wei, 204.
5. Ibid., 208.
6. Ibid., 210.
7. Fenby, 544.
8. Spence, 664.
9. Nathan, 34.
10. Ibid.
11. Wei, 224-225.
12. Ibid., 136-142.

5   Bao Tong's Fall

1. Salisbury, *The New Emperors: China in the Era of Mao and Deng* (New York: Avon Books, 1992), 30.
2. Fenby, 521.
3. Nathan, 37-38.
4. Ibid., 101.
5. Ibid., 128.
6. Zhao Dingxin, *The Power of Tiananmen: State-Society Relations and the 1989 Beijing Student Movement* (Chicago: The University of Chicago Press, 2001), 126.
7. Calhoun, 14.
8. Ibid., 16.
9. Fenby, 574.
10. Ziyang Zhao, *Prisoner of the State* (London: Simon & Schuster, 2009), 256-257.
11. Ibid., 257.
12. Ibid., 258.
13. Ibid., 259.
14. Ibid.
15. Ibid., 260.
16. Ibid., 251.
17. Ibid., 17.

6 Wang Dan's Shooting Star
1. Calhoun, 51.
2. Dingxin Zhao, 85-86.
3. Zhang, 12
4. Ibid., 16-17.
5. Calhoun, 34.
6. Ibid., 29-30.
7. Fenby, 584-585.
8. Calhoun, 30-31.
9. Ibid., 36.
10. Zhang, 26.
11. Zhao D., 148.
12. Zhang, 26-32.
13. Calhoun, 39.
14. Zhang, 38-39.
15. Ibid., 46.
16. Ibid., 50.
17. Ibid., 53.
18. Ibid., 73.
19. Fenby, 598.
20. Zhang, 71.
21. Ibid., 107.
22. Ibid.
23. Fenby, 607.
24. Zhang, 166.
25. Fenby, 606.
26. Zhang, 189-190.
27. Calhoun, 81.
28. Ibid., 77.
29. Zhang, 265.
30. Ibid., 358.
31. Ibid., 361-362.

7 Deng Xiaoping's Victory
1. Zhang, 430.
2. Fenby, 641.
3. Ibid.
4. Zhang, 313.

8 Han Dongfang's Perseverance
1. For a good survey of the impact of the Internet in China, see Pierre Haski's *Internet et la Chine* (Paris: Éditions du Seuil, 2008).
2. Yu Keping, *Democracy Is a Good Thing: Essays on Politics, Society, and Culture in Contemporary China* (Washington: Brookings Institution Press, 2009).
3. Andrew Nathan, "China's Political Trajectory: What Are the Chinese Saying?" in Li Cheng, ed., *China's Changing Political Landscape: Prospects for Democracy* (Washington: Brookings Institution Press, 2008), 29.
4. *The Building of Political Democracy in China* white paper is accessible on several websites, including: www.china.org.cn/english/2005/Oct/145718.htm, accessed October 1, 2012.
5. Ibid.
6. Jacques DeLisle, "Legalization Without Democratization in China under Hu Jintao" in Li Cheng, ed., 197.
7. David Shambaugh, *China's Communist Party: Atrophy and Adaptation* (Washington: Woodrow Wilson Center Press, 2008), 119-120.

9 Xi Jinping's China
1. See American academic Kellee S. Tsai's inquiry into three hundred Chinese entrepreneurs and executives, *Capitalism without Democracy: The Private Sector in*

Contemporary China (Ithaca: Cornell University Press, 2007). A more recent investigation of two thousand Chinese entrepreneurs reveals that a large majority of them reject the idea of multi-party elections in China: Jie Chen and Bruce Dickson, *Allies of the State: China's Private Entrepreneurs and Democratic Change* (Cambridge, Massachusetts: Harvard University Press, 2010).

2. Elizabeth J. Perry and Merle Goldman, eds. *Grassroots Political Reform in Contemporary China* (Cambridge, Massachusetts: Harvard University Press, 2007), 2. See also Gunter Schubert, "La démocratie peut-elle coexister avec le parti unique? Pour une appreciation nuance des elections villageoises et cantonales en Chine" in Delmas-Marty and Will, op. cit. 713-733.

3. Shambaugh, 52.

4. Yang Yao, "The End of the Beijing Consensus," *Foreign Affairs*, February 2, 2010.

5. Pei Minxin, "Will the Chinese Communist Party Survive the Crisis?" *Foreign Affairs*, March 12, 2009.

6. American sinologist Andrew Nathan coined the expression.

7. Pei, op. cit., 15.

8. See Larry Diamond, "The Democratic Rollback: The Resurgence of the Predatory State," *Foreign Affairs*, 87, no. 2 (March/April 2008): 36-48.

9. The expression is by Yuan Zhiming, the young philosopher who had to leave China after Tiananmen Square. Zhang, 522.

Select Bibliography

Publisher's note: Titles preceded by an asterisk refer to quotations in the text that have received the consent of various publishers who hold the copyright.

Barnouin, Barbara, and Yu Changgen. *Zhou En-lai: A Political Life*. Hong Kong: The Chinese University Press, 2006.

Béja, Jean-Philippe. "À la recherche d'une ombre chinoise : Le mouvement pour la démocratie en Chine (1919-2004)." *L'Histoire immédiate*. Paris: Éditions du Seuil, 2004.

Bell, Daniel A. *China's New Confucianism: Politics and Everyday Life in a Changing Society*. Princeton: Princeton University Press, 2008.

Bergère, Marie-Claire. *Sun Yat-sen*. Stanford: Stanford University Press, 1998.

Bergsten, C. Fred, Bates Gill, Nicholas R. Lardy, and Derek J. Mitchell. *China: The Balance Sheet: What the World Needs to Know Now About the Emerging Superpower*. New York: Public Affairs, 2006.

*Calhoun, Craig. *Neither Gods nor Emperors: Students and the Struggle for Democracy in China*. Berkeley and Los Angeles: University of California Press, 1997.

Chang, June, and Jon Halliday. *Mao*. Paris: Gallimard, 2005.

Chen Guidi and Wu Chuntao. *Will the Boat Sink the River? The Life of China's Peasants*. London: Public Affairs, 2006.

Cheng, Anne, ed. *La pensée en Chine aujourd'hui*. Paris: Gallimard, 2007.

Delmas-Marty, Mireille, and Pierre-Étienne Will, eds. *La Chine et la démocratie*. Paris: Fayard, 2007.

Diamond, Larry. *The Spirit of Democracy. The Struggle to Build Free Societies Throughout the World*. New York: Henry Holt and Company, 2008.

Dunn, John. *Setting the People Free: The Story of Democracy*. London: Atlantic Books, 2005.

Fenby, Jonathan. *Alliance: The Inside Story of How Roosevelt, Stalin & Churchill Won One War and Began Another*. London: Pocket Books, 2006.

*Fenby, Jonathan. *The Penguin History of Modern China: The Fall and Rise of a Great Power, 1850-2008*. London: Penguin Books, 2008.

Fraser, John. *The Chinese: Portrait of a People*. Don Mills: Collins Publishers, 1981.

Gilley, Bruce. *China's Democratic Future: How It Will Happen and Where It Will Lead*. New York: Columbia University Press, 2004.

Haski, Pierre. *Internet et la Chine*. Paris: Éditions du Seuil, 2008.

Holzman, Marie, and Chen Yan, eds. *Écrits édifiants et curieux sur la Chine du XXIᵉ siècle: Voyage à travers la pensée chinoise contemporaine*. La Tour d'Aigues: Éditions de l'Aube, 2004.

Johnson, Ian. *Wild Grass: China's Revolution from Below*. London: Penguin Books, 2004.

Kristof, Nicholas D., and Sheryl WuDunn. *China Wakes: The Struggle for the Soul of a Rising Power*. New York: Vintage Books, 1995.

Kuhn, Robert Lawrence. *How China's Leaders Think*. Singapore: John Wiley & Sons (Asia), 2010.

Lam, Willy Wo-Lap. *The Era of Zhao Ziyang. Power Struggle in China, 1986-88*. Hong Kong: A.B Books, 1989.

*Lary, Diana. *China's Republic*. Cambridge: Cambridge University Press, 2007.

Li Cheng, ed. *China's Changing Political Landscape: Prospects for Democracy*. Washington: Brookings Institution Press, 2008.

Lieberthal, Kenneth. *Governing China: From Revolution Through Reform*. New York: W.W. Norton & Company, 2004.

MacMillan, Margaret. *Nixon and Mao: The Week That Changed the World*. Toronto: Random House, 2007.

Mann, James. *The China Fantasy: How Our Leaders Explain Away Chinese Repression*. New York: Viking, 2007.

Nathan, Andrew J. *Chinese Democracy*. Berkeley and Los Angeles: University of California Press, 1985.

Nathan, Andrew J., and Bruce Gilley. *China's New Rulers: The Secret Files*. New York: New York Review Books, 2003.

O'Brien, Kevin J., and Liangjiang Li. *Rightful Resistance in Rural China*. Cambridge: Cambridge University Press, 2006.

Peerenboom, Randal. *China Modernizes: Threat to the West or Model for the Rest?* Oxford: Oxford University Press, 2007.

Pei Minxin. *China's Trapped Transition: The Limits of Developmental Autocracy*. Cambridge, Massachusetts: Harvard University Press, 2006.

Perry, Elizabeth J., and Merle Goldman, eds. *Grassroots Political Reform in Contemporary China*. Cambridge, Massachusetts: Harvard University Press, 2007.

Pietra, Régine. *La Chine et le confucianisme aujourd'hui*. Paris: Le Félin/Poche, 2008.

*Salisbury, Harrison E. *The New Emperors: China in the Era of Mao and Deng*. New York: Avon Books, 1992.

*Shambaugh, David. *China's Communist Party: Atrophy and Adaptation*. Washington: Woodrow Wilson Centre Press, 2008.

Shi, Tianjian. *Political Participation in Beijing*. Cambridge, Massachusetts: Harvard University Press, 1997.

Shirk, Susan L. *China: Fragile Superpower: How China's Internal Politics Could Derail Its Peaceful Rise*. Oxford: Oxford University Press, 2007.

Snow, Edgar. *Red Star Over China: The Classic Account of the Birth of Chinese Communism*. New York: Grove Press, 1968.

Spence, Jonathan D. *The Search for Modern China*. New York: W.W. Norton & Company, 1990.

Tsai, Kellee S. *Capitalism Without Democracy: The Private Sector in Contemporary China*. Ithaca: Cornell University Press, 2007.

Tsai, Lily L. *Accountability without Democracy: Solidarity Groups and Public Goods Provision in Rural China*. Cambridge: Cambridge University Press, 2007.

Wang Hui. *China's New Order: Society, Politics, and Economy in Transition*. Cambridge, Massachusetts: Harvard University Press, 2003.

Wang Juntao. *Reverse Course: Political Neo-conservatism and Regime Stability in Post-Tiananmen China*. Saarbrücken: VDM Verlag Dr. Müller, 2008.

Wei Jingsheng. *The Courage to Stand Alone: Letters from Prison and Other Writings*. New York: Penguin, 1997.

Yu Keping. *Democracy Is a Good Thing: Essays on Politics, Society, and Culture in Contemporary China*. Washington: Brookings Institution Press, 2009.

Yu-Lan Fung. *A Short History of Chinese Philosophy: A Systematic Account of Chinese Thought from Its Origins to the Present Day*. New York: The Free Press, 1976.

Zhang Boli. *Escape From China: The Long Journey from Tiananmen to Freedom*. New York: Washington Square Press, 1998.

Zhang Liang, Andrew J. Nathan, and Perry Link, eds. *The Tiananmen Papers: The Chinese Leadership's Decision to Use Force Against Their Own People — In Their Own Words*. New York: Public Affairs, 2001.

*Zhao Dingxin. *The Power of Tiananmen: State-Society Relations and the 1989 Beijing Student Movement*. Chicago: The University of Chicago Press, 2001.

Zhao Ziyang. *Prisoner of the State*. London: Simon & Schuster, 2009.

Index